FIND YOUR FEDERAL JOB FIT

Janet M. Ruck and Karol Taylor

D0957888

jist
Works
America's Career Publisher®

Find Your Federal Job Fit

© 2012 by Janet M. Ruck and Karol Taylor

Published by JIST Works, an imprint of JIST Publishing
875 Montreal Way
St. Paul, MN 55102

Phone: 800-648-JIST   E-mail: info@jist.com   Website: www.jist.com

Also by the authors: *Guide to America's Federal Jobs*

Visit www.jist.com for information on JIST, tables of contents, sample pages, and more details on our many products.

Quantity discounts are available for JIST products. Please call 800-648-5478 or visit www.jist.com for a free catalog and more information.

Acquisitions and Development Editor: Susan Pines
Cover Designer: Alan Evans
Interior Designer and Layout: Aleata Halbig
Proofreader: Jeanne Clark
Indexer: Cheryl Ann Lenser

Printed in the United States of America

16 15 14 13 12 11   9 8 7 6 5 4 3 2 1

Library of Congress Cataloging-in-Publication Data

Ruck, Janet M.
  Find your federal job fit / Janet M. Ruck and Karol Taylor.
    p. cm.
  Includes index.
  ISBN 978-1-59357-834-3 (alk. paper)
  1. Civil service positions--United States. I. Taylor, Karol. II. Title.
  JK716.R85 2011
  351.73023--dc23

2011027152

We have been careful to provide accurate information throughout this book, but it is possible that errors and omissions have been introduced. Please consider this in making any career plans or other important decisions. Trust your own judgment above all else and in all things.

ISBN 978-1-59357-834-3

TABLE OF CONTENTS

FOREWORD

I recently completed a two-year work experience within NASA, and it opened my eyes to the world of federal employment opportunities. In addition to feeling patriotism and purpose, I learned the value, pride, and importance of federal employment.

Even in a changing economy, federal opportunities exist and are overlooked and misunderstood. The federal government needs the best and brightest to deliver solutions in agencies that focus on issues from Main Street to outer space. These needed workers include recent graduates, veterans eligible for hiring preferences, and people with disabilities. With federal jobs come personal development and learning opportunities as good as most graduate schools, plus good salaries and job security.

Fortunately, this book lands at the right time when many workers feel nervously employed; discouraged; and eager to find some certainty, a second chance, or a new purpose. Janet Ruck and Karol Taylor's work offers essential insights about the federal government as an employer, as well as targeted strategies to get hired by agencies most people cannot name. Their wisdom from years of rich career consulting to federal workers and their exceptional federal experience make them experienced tour guides in a land of rich job opportunity.

Ruck and Taylor's work addresses needs identified through research:

- *Employees need greater career assistance but are not accessing the best or most useful resources...too few go to trained career specialists.* The authors are skilled career consultants who offer easy-to-read and self-directed activities that accelerate career awareness and exploration.

- *Data shows that adults look to job postings but have little information about the career-planning process. Find Your Federal Job Fit* offers such a roadmap.

- *Segments of the workforce, such as veterans, the disabled, and those leaving military service, have historically faced greater challenges in finding full-time employment.* The authors offer clear instruction in networking, targeting application materials, and preparing for behavioral and situational interviews. This information is essential for moving beyond generic resumes and approaches.

- *Significant numbers of workers are less than fully satisfied with their jobs, and many continue to report that they wish they had known more when they got started in their present career.* Ruck and Taylor's introduction to federal departments and top fields where the government is hiring offers clarity about the federal workplace and a focus beyond an "I'll take a job with anyone" job search.

There is much to be concerned about regarding America's future. Yet job seekers and career counselors can be optimistic that constancy exists in the career-planning process described in this book. Ruck and Taylor offer hope to readers and clarity to counselors on how to distill assets and align them with the federal workplace.

Congratulations to Janet Ruck and Karol Taylor for a great service and for a wonderful resource for maximizing talent and doing purposeful federal work.

Rich Feller, Ph.D.

Professor of Counseling and Career Development and Distinguished Teaching Scholar, Colorado State University

President-Elect, National Career Development Association

INTRODUCTION

An interesting byproduct of the current economic downturn has been a renewed interest in federal employment. For the past few years, the federal government has made steady gains as the employer of choice. Uncle Sam is now a more attractive option.

This book was born out of our experiences as career consultants to federal employees and as retired federal employees. We found that many of our colleagues and clients toiled in federal jobs that were not the right match for them. Often these individuals could not pinpoint their ideal job, primarily because they were unclear about their interests and ideals. Sometimes they were unaware of their skills and what they had to offer the federal government as an employee.

In addition, the federal application process, which is unlike any other, can be cumbersome and confusing at times. It is based on a set of laws and regulations that were written for a specific purpose. Over time, layers of new laws were added. Eventually they created a morass of rules that now make up the federal hiring system.

We wrote this book as a way to reach as many federal job seekers as possible. *Find Your Federal Job Fit* is designed as a self-coaching guide for anyone considering the federal government for a career. Rather than follow the adage to take any federal job to get your foot in the door, you want to find a job that fits you. We want to assist you in your search for federal work that matches your skills, interests, and talents.

If you are a current federal employee, and you have been frustrated in your efforts to find meaningful work, this book is for you as well.

Finally, if you do not understand federal hiring but would like a fulfilling federal career, this book is your answer. It will help you to identify and avoid the pitfalls often made by novice federal job seekers. This book can be your federal job search guidance system. Use it as a workbook. Write in it and make notes—it's *your* book! Following it carefully will help you find the way to your best federal job fit.

How This Book Is Organized

The book is divided into five parts:

- "Part I: Understanding Federal Job Search Basics" overviews the most common mistakes that federal job seekers make. It also covers the federal government as an employer.

- "Part II: Understanding Yourself" is a career-planning resource to help you conduct self-assessments and develop a career identity.

- "Part III: Becoming Familiar with Federal Opportunities" introduces you to federal departments and federal jobs. It explains the top skills wanted by the federal government in its employees.

- "Part IV: Translating YOU to the Federal Government" helps you to begin matching yourself to federal jobs, explains how to enhance your skills for federal jobs of interest, and guides you in developing a career plan.

- "Part V: Getting a Federal Job" highlights the best methods for landing the federal job of your dreams.

- Appendixes provide helpful federal job–seeking tools, plus federal job information for new graduates, transitioning military, and people with disabilities.

Best Wishes in Finding Your Federal Career Fit

We wish you the best in your pursuit of meaningful work in the federal government. A federal career is truly an opportunity for you to serve your country as well as use your talents.

Don't leave your career to chance. Maximize your contributions and fulfill your mission by knowing who you are and what you offer and matching them to the right federal job!

AS KINGFISHERS CATCH FIRE

As kingfishers catch fire, dragonflies dráw fláme;

As tumbled over rim in roundy wells

Stones ring; like each tucked string tells, each hung bell's

Bow swung finds tongue to fling out broad its name;

Each mortal thing does one thing and the same:

Deals out that being indoors each one dwells;

Selves — goes itself; myself it speak and spells,

Crying Whát I do is me: for that I came.

Gerard Manley Hopkins

PART I

UNDERSTANDING FEDERAL JOB SEARCH BASICS

CHAPTER 1

11 COMMON MISTAKES THAT FEDERAL JOB SEEKERS MAKE

Federal job seekers flock to USAJOBS.gov, the official federal government jobs website, to identify positions they might like. These job seekers submit applications and wait. Often nothing happens. They try again. Still nothing happens. Savvy job hunters find someone in the know to show them the ropes. Others throw up their hands in frustration and walk away.

Here are the 11 most common mistakes that federal job seekers make. These mistakes often cost well-qualified applicants their opportunity to obtain a federal job.

1. Beginning the Federal Job Search Without Target Occupations

On any given day, USAJOBS lists more than 5,000 federal job openings. Without a job target or targets, you will find that it is virtually impossible to know where and how to focus your search. Time spent in self-assessment and career exploration can pay dividends in seeking and finding a federal job that fits. This book helps you with that process.

2. Taking Any Federal Job to Get Your Foot in the Door of the Federal Government

Taking any federal job to get your foot in the door is not solid advice. Lateral transfers (that is, job mobility at the same grade and salary) often are difficult to obtain. Given the arduous hiring process, federal managers are reluctant to allow employees to move from their current positions. In fact, the law states that job transfer is required only in the case of promotion. In other words, it is not easy to move around after you have been hired.

The best strategy, therefore, is to follow a job search plan that stems from your career exploration. It will streamline your federal job search as well as provide you with a more satisfying career after you have been hired into the federal government.

3. Narrowing Your Job Search Geographically by Focusing Only on Washington, D.C.

The majority of federal jobs are located outside Washington, D.C. In fact, only 15 percent of federal jobs are in D.C. You may be overlooking many opportunities by restricting your search to the nation's capital.

4. Overlooking Networking as a Powerful Federal Job Search Tool

Many federal job seekers focus only on online sites and electronic applications. Although federal law requires that the federal application process adhere to strict guidelines, you can find out about federal opportunities in many ways. Chapter 10 discusses the best ways to network to get known and noticed by federal hiring managers. It is always important to distinguish yourself in the crowded federal marketplace.

5. Applying with a Generic Resume

It is critical that you develop a targeted resume for every type of position for which you are applying. A one-size-fits-all resume robs you of the opportunity to market your qualifications in the context of the job. It can take an average of 10 hours to apply for a federal job if you analyze the vacancy announcement carefully and construct a resume that is specifically targeted to the announcement.

6. Not Promoting Yourself

Many applicants fear bragging and operate under the outdated yet prevalent myth that selling themselves in a job search campaign is not respectable. However, in a competitive marketplace, applicants who have the ability to toot their own horn are likely to get noticed, interviewed, and hired.

It is equally important to bolster your claims with facts and stories that illustrate your successes. To sell yourself with substance, we recommend that you use the "CCAR" method:

- Context—describe the environment

- Challenge—describe the situation or problem you confronted

- Action—describe what measures you took to resolve the problem

- Result—describe the outcome of your actions in quantifiable terms

By following the CCAR approach, you substantiate your claims that you are the most qualified for a job through real-life examples with results. In addition, success stories add interest and depth to your application, which otherwise could be a lackluster accounting of facts and dates.

7. Applying for Everything

A wise investment of time is ensuring that you are qualified and eligible for a federal position before you assemble your application. You are wasting your time by applying for a position without sufficiently analyzing the vacancy announcement. Often federal job seekers quickly scan the overview section of an announcement, maybe quickly peruse the duties section, and then decide that they are qualified to apply.

8. Not Spending Enough Time Targeting Application Materials to Your Audience

Applying for a federal job requires a definite commitment of time and energy. Give yourself a chance to get an interview by analyzing the vacancy announcement and writing for your audience. In the federal online application process, you are writing for three audiences:

- Electronic scanner, which scans and sorts the keywords that are listed in the vacancy announcement

- Human resources staff, who determine your qualifications according to the vacancy announcement

- Hiring official, who determines who will be interviewed

Take the time to specifically target your resume and other application materials to the position. You must address the needs and desires of your audiences. You must demonstrate, through your written application materials, why you are the most qualified applicant for the position.

9. Choosing Jobs Based on Salary Only

If the salary for a federal position seems low compared to what you earned in the private sector, consider the many benefits of federal employment. Do not limit your search by the pay listed on the vacancy announcement. Focus on the qualifications section of the announcement to determine whether the position is within your scope of experience and skills.

10. Applying Only for Jobs on USAJOBS

In addition to applying for jobs through USAJOBS, use other sites and other methods to learn about and apply for federal jobs. Federal law does not require that vacancies be posted on USAJOBS; the law requires only that jobs be advertised. Some federal agencies post their jobs on their own websites only. Commercial sites that list federal jobs include www.avuecentral. com and www.indeed.com.

In addition, don't overlook the personal approach of learning about federal jobs through networking and informational interviews. Join a professional association to meet people in your field who may be able to assist you in looking for a federal job. This approach is explored in chapter 10.

11. Misrepresenting Background and Experience

Never lie on or embellish your resume or any application materials. It is certainly important to sell yourself, but do so authentically and honestly. If you are hired based on any misrepresentation in your application, you can expect to be summarily terminated if it is discovered. This point includes your education and where you received it. Be aware that you may be subjected to a background investigation as a new federal hire. All information in your application may be verified.

Closing Thoughts

This book will help you avoid the most common mistakes in federal job-seeking.

CHAPTER 2

THE FEDERAL GOVERNMENT AS AN EMPLOYER

E ven in a down or recovering economy, the federal government continues to hire! With up to 2 million employees, it is the nation's largest employer. With so many jobs, the government has excellent bartering power and can offer you great benefits. Plus, 85 percent of federal employees work outside the Washington, D.C., metropolitan area, so federal jobs can be found across the country and around the world.

Overview of Federal Employment

The U.S. Department of Labor's Bureau of Labor Statistics (BLS) provides an overview of federal employment at www. bls.gov/oco/cg/cgs041.htm. A key point made on the website is that a substantial number of federal employees will be eligible to retire during the upcoming decade. Even if the federal labor force gets downsized, right-sized, and outsourced, many federal jobs still will need to be filled. Based on BLS information, plenty of federal jobs should be available for the foreseeable future.

Three Branches of the Federal Government

The federal government infrastructure has three branches: legislative, judicial, and executive. According to the BLS, the legislative branch employs about 1 percent of all federal civilian workers, and the judicial branch about 2 percent. Because it has the broadest range of responsibilities, the executive branch hires approximately 97 percent of all federal civilian employees (excluding postal workers who are not considered members of the federal civilian workforce).

You will learn more about federal agencies and opportunities in chapter 5.

Categories of Federal Jobs

Federal jobs are placed in two major groups, civil service or military service. The term *civil service* applies to any federal job where the applicant competes and qualifies based on his or her work experience. The job is not awarded through patronage or as a personal favor; it is earned through the applicant's knowledge, skills, and abilities. We focus on civil service jobs in this book.

Civil service jobs fall into one of three basic categories, or "services." They are the Competitive Service, the Excepted Service, and the Senior Executive Service:

- The Competitive Service includes jobs primarily in the executive branch of the government.

- The Excepted Service includes most of the positions in the legislative branch and the judicial branch of the government, as well as positions in the Central Intelligence

Agency, the Federal Bureau of Investigation, and other agencies that have been excepted from the civil service laws because of their confidential, policy-determining, or policy-advocating character.

- The Senior Executive Service includes executive and managerial positions that do not require appointment by the President with Senate confirmation.

Other differences among the three services are in hiring procedures and job protections. In the Competitive Service, hiring procedures, promotion requirements, and job qualification standards are prescribed by law or by the U.S. Office of Personnel Management (OPM) and apply to all agencies. In the Excepted Service, only basic requirements are prescribed by law or regulation, and each agency develops specific requirements and procedures for its own jobs. Another difference between employment in the Competitive Service and the Excepted Service is the ability of Competitive Service employees to achieve "competitive" or "career" status.

Competitive/career status is conveyed automatically to Competitive Service employees who successfully complete a required term of service (typically three years of continuous full-time federal employment). Because many vacancies advertised by federal agencies are open only to federal employees with competitive/career status, Competitive Service employees often are considered to have greater mobility to apply for jobs at other federal agencies. In addition, employees with competitive/career status may be hired to other positions in the Competitive Service without having to compete with members of the general public through an open vacancy announcement.

Federal Occupational Series

Each federal job announcement has a four-digit code listed under "series and grade" in the overview section. You can locate this code between the letters "GS" and the grade for which the job is posted. Those four numbers represent the occupational series under which the job is classified. There are currently 22 general occupations, each divided into a number of different series. To view the federal job classification series designations, go to www.opm.gov/fedclass/html/gsseries.asp.

Understanding how the occupational series system works is important to your federal job search. Each series requires specialized skills. Armed with these skills, you meet the qualifications requirements for the job. Without these skills, you are not qualified to apply for the job. More about the federal occupational series is discussed in chapter 7.

Office of Personnel Management

OPM is the human resources (HR) agency for the executive branch of the federal government. OPM provides policy direction to other agencies; a central portal for federal job announcements (that is, USAJOBS); investigation services to agencies seeking to hire individuals; retirement and insurance benefits to federal employees, retirees, and their families; and HR services to other agencies. Explore the OPM website at www.opm.gov.

Benefits of Federal Employees

Each new federal hire is offered the same choice of benefits. OPM provides oversight for federal benefit programs.

Options for benefits include the following:

- Comprehensive health and life insurance
- Competitive salaries
- Generous retirement programs
- 10 paid holidays
- Sick leave and vacation time
- Flexible work environment and alternative work schedules
- Paid employment-related training and education
- Possible student loan repayment
- Payment of licenses, certification, and academic degrees as applicable
- Bonuses
- Incentives
- Awards as appropriate for the job

 "A true measure of your worth includes all the benefits others have gained from your success."

Cullen Hightower, author and political conservative

Here is more detail on federal job benefits:

- Federal employees are able to enroll in health, dental, vision, life insurance, and flexible spending health accounts and to apply for long-term care insurance. The federal government pays 72 percent of the monthly premium for health benefits, whether for the employee or for family. Federal group life insurance is a term policy, so premiums are low when you are young and increase noticeably as you age.

- OPM's salary table is updated on January 1 of each year to reflect an annual cost of living allowance (COLA), if any. The link to the salary table is located to the right on OPM's home page, www.opm.gov, under Most Requested Tasks/View Salaries and Wages.

- Joining the Federal Employees Retirement System (FERS) is highly recommended. FERS combines retirement benefits from three different sources: a Basic Benefit Plan, Social Security, and the Thrift Savings Plan (TSP). Federal agencies match 1 percent of your basic pay each pay period and deposit it into your TSP account.

- Federal employees have 10 established public holidays: New Year's Day, Martin Luther King Jr. Birthday, President's Day, Memorial Day, Independence Day, Labor Day, Columbus Day, Veteran's Day, Thanksgiving, and Christmas.

- Full-time employees earn a half day (four hours) of sick leave for each biweekly pay period.

- For each biweekly pay period, full-time employees also earn a half day of annual leave the first 3 years of employment, and six hours after that until they reach 15 years of service. After 15 years, federal employees earn eight hours of leave for each pay period.

- The standard federal workday is 8.5 hours from the time the employee arrives until the time he or she leaves. Many federal agencies offer flexi-time, where an employee can arrive any time between 6:30 a.m. to 10 a.m. and leave 8.5 hours later. If an agency offers alternative work schedules and flexible work environments, it might offer 1) four 10-hour days per week and a three-day weekend, and/or 2) the "five-four-nine" program: eight nine-hour days, one eight-hour day, and an extra day off every other week during a pay period. When they opt for either of these alternatives, employees must be at work three core days per week: Tuesday, Wednesday, and Thursday. Also, some federal agencies offer flexi-place. They allow their employees to telecommute from home. When flexi-place is an option, employees sometimes telecommute on core workdays. There's a lot of flexibility for attendance in the federal workplace, but your time is closely monitored, so excellent performance is the highest priority.

- Some agencies offer a full hour for lunch, and some a half hour. Decisions about lunchtime breaks depend on the agency and the type of work performed there.

- The federal government pays for specific employment-related training and education. Recipients of such funding sign a training agreement, which is an agreement to serve in the agency three times the length of the training period. Payment of licenses, certification, and academic degrees can also be funded by federal agencies if the agency chooses. Again, recipients must sign a training agreement for some of these expenses. Student loan payment is optional for federal agencies and must be negotiated on receiving a job offer. You will want to receive a written agreement, which should guarantee your student loan payment. A verbal agreement may not provide as much protection, because people change jobs, and situations change.

- Agencies can use referral bonuses and incentives to support recruitment and hiring. Relocation incentives are given when the agency needs an employee to move to a geographic area where a position is likely to be difficult to fill. Retention incentives are paid to employees with unusually high or unique qualifications or to meet a special need of the agency. Four types of awards can be given to federal employees: lump-sum cash awards, honorary awards, informal recognition awards, and time-off awards. Money is attached to some of these awards.

Location of Federal Jobs

You can use Browse Jobs on USAJOBS to determine the location of federal job openings. Approximately 15 percent of federal jobs are located in the Washington, D.C., area, which means that 85 percent are located elsewhere, mostly in the U.S. More than 44,000 civil service jobs employees are located overseas. However, most agency headquarters for the 15 federal departments and 100-plus agencies are located in the metropolitan D.C. area. Most federal agencies have regional offices throughout the country.

 "The two most important requirements for major success are: first, being in the right place at the right time, and second, doing something about it."

Ray Kroc, creator of the McDonald's empire

States with regional offices include California, Colorado, Georgia, Illinois, Missouri, Massachusetts, New York, Pennsylvania, Texas, and Washington. States with the highest number of federal employees include California, Florida, Georgia, Maryland, New York, Ohio, Pennsylvania, Texas, Virginia, and Washington.

Closing Thoughts

As you can see, federal benefits are excellent, and federal employment is available around the globe.

PART II

UNDERSTANDING YOURSELF

CHAPTER 3

KNOWING YOURSELF—
WHO ARE YOU, REALLY?

You are more than just the sum of your salary, benefits, and other compensation. You are an individual with skills, talents, and expertise that the federal government needs.

Finding a Meaningful Federal Career

So many occupations, so little time! Taking the time to discover the federal occupations that fit you is an investment that will pay dividends throughout your career.

Many people don't take the time to explore careers that resonate with them. In the rush to find a job and earn a living, people often find themselves settling for anything, perhaps thinking that "I'll do this just for a while, and then I'll find something else." Or job seekers downplay the significance of finding work that fits them, thinking "It's just a job; I'll find my meaning elsewhere." However, rushing to a resolution and minimizing the consequences of a career decision can translate into lifelong unhappiness. Why? Because people often find themselves trapped in federal jobs that don't fit.

"Choose a job you love and you will never work a day in your life."

Confucius, philosopher

Activities You Enjoy

Here are some questions to ask yourself as you prepare to find the right federal career fit. Write down the first answer that pops into your head, without censor or edit. The purpose of the questions is to guide your career thinking in the direction you choose and to consider the activities that enthuse you and motivate you.

As you explore the areas of your life that interest you, it is important to consider any and all possibilities. You will consider whether they are realistic for a federal career later in the book. For now, please do not rule anything out.

What types of activities do you enjoy?

_____

_____

_____

_____

_____

_____

_____

_____

If you were given the opportunity to do anything you wanted, what would you choose?

_____

_____

_____

_____

_____

If you had an unexpected day off, with no commitments or appointments, how would you spend your time?

_____

_____

_____

_____

_____

What would you do for free, without regard for compensation, solely for the love of it?

_____

_____

_____

_____

_____

Activities You Enjoyed in the Past

What are some aspects of your life that you enjoyed in the past? Was it being outside for hours planting in your garden? Maybe your favorite projects involved the indoors. Or perhaps you were encouraging someone to learn. Were you an adventurer, looking for new challenges or developing a new skill on your own? Did you have a thirst for knowledge? What activities made you feel alive?

In the space below, list activities that you enjoyed in your past. Don't think about whether they will earn you money or what you can do with the activities. Focus on those activities that brought you joy merely for the sake of doing them.

I have liked these activities:

_____

_____

_____

_____

_____

Your Values

When you consider the type of federal work that you want to pursue, it is important to think about what matters to you. Values can be thought of as the beliefs and attitudes that you hold in high esteem. At their core, values are fundamental, because in large part they form the foundation of who you are as an individual.

In assessing your values, consider which aspects of your life make it worth living and create a sense of purpose and fulfillment, without which you would be merely existing, not living with vitality and vibrancy. Without these aspects, you might feel like a shell, as if your soul were disengaged from your body.

"Wherever you go, go with all your heart."

Confucius, philosopher

You make choices each and every day based on your values. Have you ever stopped to identify and name your values so that they become and remain the substance of your work? As you consider your values, many questions can help you frame your recognition of them.

Consider the following: What is important to have as an integral part of your life? Is it recognition, gratitude, knowledge, or approval? A workplace with people you enjoy or people who make you laugh? Spend a few moments gathering your ideas and writing down what is important for you to include in your life and work.

_____

_____

_____

_____

_____

The following values assessment will also be helpful in your career decision-making.

What I Value Most

From this list of values (both work and personal), check the 10 that are the most important to you as guides for how to behave or as components of a valued way of life. Feel free to add any values of your own to this list.

I value

_____ Owning a fine home

_____ Wearing fashionable clothes

_____ Having freeing relationships

_____ Having harmonious relationships

_____ Having confrontive relationships

_____ Having good food and drink

_____ Having cars (or boats or planes)

_____ Earning and having money

_____ Traveling and seeing the world

_____ Having challenges

_____ Having financial security

_____ Living the rich life

_____ Having a close family

_____ Having steady employment

_____ Using my creativity

_____ Having a good marriage

_____ Having close friends

_____ Being productive

_____ Feeling my life counts

_____ Helping others

_____ Being a hard worker

_____ Using my skills and abilities

_____ Continuing self-discovery

_____ Being close to nature

_____ Feeling my work really counts

_____ Empowering others

_____ Using my mind

_____ Working for important causes

_____ Being safe

_____ Having a good fight

_____ Taking risks

(continued)

(continued)

What I Value Most

_____ Accepting physical or athletic risks (challenges)

_____ Having cultural opportunities

_____ Stretching myself emotionally

_____ Being my own person

_____ Being in a position of authority

_____ Stretching myself mentally

_____ Expressing kindness and love

_____ Having possessions of value

_____ Fostering respect for all

_____ Using my body

_____ Learning and gaining knowledge

_____ Being spiritual

_____ Being an authority in my field

_____ Getting and using power

_____ Having fame and recognition

_____ Participating in religious or club activities

_____ Having a relationship with God

_____ Being politically active

_____ Being free and independent

_____ Having honesty and integrity

_____ Having a meaningful love relationship

_____ Being in front of the crowd

_____ Working independently

_____ Playing and being playful

_____ Having good health

_____ Having a long life

_____ Working with a team or group

_____ Resting and relaxing

_____ Having career satisfaction

_____ Having adventure and excitement

_____ Supporting justice for all

_____ Having and making order

_____ Having new and unique experiences

_____ Living on the fast track

_____ Appreciating beauty

(continued)

(continued)

What I Value Most

_____ Other _____

_____ Other _____

_____ Other _____

Adapted by Karol Taylor from Fontelle Gilbert's values assessment developed at Prince George's Community College. Used with permission.

Your Special Skills

A skill is an observable action that indicates aptitude and ability. Dictionary.com defines skill as the ability, coming from one's knowledge, practice, aptitude, and so on, to do something well. For example: *Carpentry was one of his many skills.*

Some career experts estimate that the average American worker possesses approximately 700 skills. Refer to appendix A for a skills assessment to help you identify what you do well.

"Because you're unique, there's something you are better at than anyone else."

Bernard Haldane, career counselor and author

You can also explore job skills at O*NET OnLine, which features job descriptions from the U.S. Department of Labor's Occupational Information Network. See this interactive website at www.onetonline.org.

Motivated Skills

Just because you excel at something doesn't mean that you enjoy it. In fact, many people choose careers based on aptitude and skill, yet they do not enjoy using these skills.

A key aspect of career satisfaction and success is engaging in work that interests you, that challenges you, and that keeps you motivated to learn and grow. It is important that you choose work that leverages and capitalizes on the skills you enjoy using. The skills that you enjoy using are *motivated skills*, because you are motivated to use them. Don't allow others to tell you that because you are good at something, you should pursue it as your life's work, if you do not enjoy using that skill.

It is crucial to find what you like and what you enjoy to create sustaining work. If you pursue federal work (or any work, for that matter) that you are good at without enjoying it, you may experience short-term success. But, for work that gives you a lifetime of success and an abundance of opportunity, use skills that you enjoy. Then you will never be bored, and you will look forward to growing these skills. In fact, the secret of success may be finding and pursuing activities that you enjoy and in which you excel.

"To find joy in work is to discover the fountain of youth."

Pearl S. Buck, author

Is there something that so engages you that you enjoy doing it over and over again? No matter where you go or what you do, sooner or later these skills get incorporated into almost everything you do. Others have commented positively on your use of these skills. Co-workers, friends, and family praise you when you engage in them. However, because they are effortless for you, you have not considered them as foundational to your success.

What are you doing when you feel this way? Describe it here:

_____

_____

_____

_____

_____

_____

Where are you doing it? It could be at work, at home, in the community, or somewhere else.

_____

_____

_____

_____

_____

_____

Unmotivated Skills

Conversely, you have skills that you don't enjoy using. Some people may be good at math, for example, but they just don't like math. For others, their talents may lie in leadership, but they don't want to be in charge. These skills are called *unmotivated skills,* because although you may excel in them, they are not what you want to do. You don't enjoy using these skills, no matter how good you are. Find a career that works for you by focusing on what you like to do, not just on what you are skilled in.

List skills you have that you don't enjoy using:

_____

_____

_____

_____

_____

_____

When did you realize that you didn't like using these skills, despite the fact that others encouraged you to pursue them?

_____

_____

_____

_____

_____

_____

When Are You "In Flow"?

Athletes call it being "in the zone," when the world seems to fade away, and there is nothing but the athlete and the sport.

The desire to improve, the quest for achievement, and the thrill of success are the activities that motivate the athlete. Being "in flow" creates an aliveness and an energy that are sustaining.

Think of a time when you were involved in a pursuit that energized you. You so enjoyed it that it didn't matter what time it was or what else was going on. You were connected to the task, and you knew you were good. Your "on" button remained engaged, because the pastime was rewarding in and of itself. Time had no meaning. What you did in one moment flowed to the next. In fact, you lost track of time. You thought of nothing except what you were involved in at the moment.

What were you doing? Describe the activity or activities. Disregard any qualms about the ability to make a living by pursuing the activity. Let go of the tendency to overthink and overanalyze your response.

_____

_____

_____

_____

_____

_____

This is flow. And, yes, you can find a federal job and earn a living by knowing and doing what keeps you in flow.

"Success is not the key to happiness. Happiness is the key to success. If you love what you are doing, you will be successful."

Albert Schweitzer, theologian and philosopher

At the Top of Your Game

There is a time when you know that you are better at what you're doing than anyone around you. You synchronize with your activity. What you are doing is so energizing that you don't want to do anything else. At this time, you are connected to your inner spirit, which manifests itself in the activity. If you were to stop and "listen" to the activity, you would discover that you are being led to your path. Do you pay attention? Or do you ignore the voice that is calling to you from your innermost self?

These are the moments in your life that, if you listened with your heart rather than your mind, you would be on a path to greatness. Do you ignore the voice that calls you to your potential? Are you choosing a life that is dictated by others' expectations and rules? Do you continually doubt who you are and what you might become?

If you do this, you often relegate yourself down a path that you didn't choose. You may become numb to your own voice and doubt your own essence. The world has created doubt in your ability to make decisions for yourself. You have become enslaved by the approval of others.

In such a scenario, you may not perform to your potential because you have turned a blind eye to maximizing your greatness. You don't know who you are, let alone what your promise is! You have abdicated yourself to the endorsement of others.

It is time, past time in fact, to discover who you really are.

 "A musician must make music, an artist must paint, a poet must write, if he is to be ultimately happy. What a man can be, he must be."

Abraham Maslow, professor

In the space that follows, describe those moments when you felt that you performed at your best. You were at the top of your game. You were unstoppable and unbeatable. What were you doing?

_____

_____

_____

_____

_____

_____

Role Models

Some people in your life inspire you. Even if they are no longer alive, they still create in you a yearning to do more and to be better than you are. They are an example of the possibilities for your life and provide a model that you can follow. Is there a person (or even a book, a movie, or something else) who gives you the desire to exceed your own expectations of yourself? Allow this person to enter your self-awareness so that you can identify what it is about him or her that moves you. These powerful messages can give you the ability to exceed the power you have experienced to this point.

Who inspires you to greatness?

_____

_____

_____

_____

_____

Why do these people inspire you? What qualities do/did they possess or what actions do/did they take that make you admire them? After you make this awareness conscious, you can willfully choose those activities that empower you. Your actions will no longer be mere accidents.

_____

_____

_____

_____

_____

_____

"If one advances confidently in the direction of his dreams and endeavors to live the life he has imagined, he will meet with success unexpected in common hours."

Henry David Thoreau, author

Occupational Daydreams

What do you dream of doing when you're gazing into the distance? Perhaps you're sitting at a red light, your thoughts far off into the future, when suddenly you see yourself involved in a career or activity that never crossed your mind before. Perhaps you are puzzled, confused, and wondering what this means. You've never envisioned yourself in this line of work, yet once you get over the feeling of confusion, you begin to get interested in it. There are definitely aspects of this occupation you might enjoy. The more you think about it, the more intrigued you become. You start to wonder why you've never thought of it before. Now that it's in your awareness, and it has become part of your consciousness, so you need to pursue it.

This is an occupational daydream, and it can give you clues to a good profession to consider. The daydream can provide a wealth of information that lay buried before. Now that it is out in the open, you may wish to follow the clues to what may be your best federal job fit.

What do you dream about doing for a career? Have you ever thought that "one day, when I retire (or some other time in the future), I will…"? Write your thoughts about your occupational daydreams:

_____

_____

_____

_____

_____

Have you ever acted on this dream? If so, what happened? If not, why not?

_____

_____

_____

_____

_____

_____

"The more assets you have and the more seeds you plant, the better your chances for achieving your goals."

David Campbell, author

Your Personality Type

The Myers-Briggs Type Indicator® (MBTI®) was developed by Katherine Myers and her daughter Isabel Myers Briggs to make the theory of psychology types described by Carl Jung understandable and useful in people's lives. The MBTI identifies people's basic preferences about perception and judgment, so that the effects of each can be used in their lives. By using the results of the MBTI, individuals can gain insight into their personalities and into how they relate to careers, relationships, learning styles, and many other issues. There are 16 personality types.

By knowing your personality preferences, you may be able to choose a career that capitalizes on your natural tendencies, thus helping you find a career that is a good fit.

Here is a list of resources to help you determine your personality type:

- www.humanmetrics.com
- www.personalitypathways.com
- www.personalitypage.com
- www.human-types.com

You can learn more about personality type by contacting a career counselor in your area.

"Make the unconscious conscious, or you will continue to call it fate."

Carl Jung, psychiatrist

Your Career Interests

Career theorist John Holland developed a theory of career choice based on six themes. According to his theory, individuals who choose work and environments that relate to their interests will be more satisfied as well as more successful. This diagram shows and defines Holland's six themes:

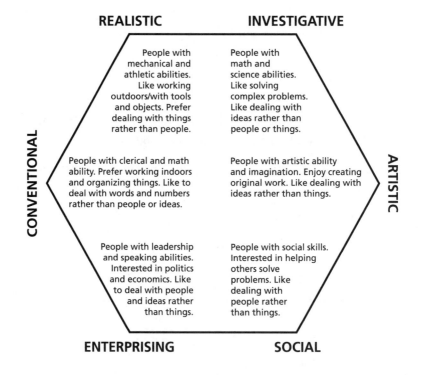

REALISTIC

People with mechanical and athletic abilities. Like working outdoors/with tools and objects. Prefer dealing with things rather than people.

INVESTIGATIVE

People with math and science abilities. Like solving complex problems. Like dealing with ideas rather than people or things.

CONVENTIONAL

People with clerical and math ability. Prefer working indoors and organizing things. Like to deal with words and numbers rather than people or ideas.

ARTISTIC

People with artistic ability and imagination. Enjoy creating original work. Like dealing with ideas rather than things.

ENTERPRISING

People with leadership and speaking abilities. Interested in politics and economics. Like to deal with people and ideas rather than things.

SOCIAL

People with social skills. Interested in helping others solve problems. Like dealing with people rather than things.

As you continue your self-exploration into federal careers that fit, it follows that if you know what your interests are, it will be easier for you to be successful. You won't get bored, there will always be something to motivate and interest you, and you will naturally make progress. The work will be fun and interesting because you are following your interests. If you focus solely on your skills, you may learn that it becomes more difficult to find fulfillment and challenge because you get bored or reach your potential quickly. But with interests, you will always seek the next challenge.

Here's a list of resources to help you determine your interests:

- www.soicc.state.nc.us/soicc/planning/c1a.htm

- http://career.missouri.edu/resources/pdfs/ Guide%20to%20Holland%20Code%20S2010.pdf

- http://career.missouri.edu/students/majors-careers/skills-interests/career-interest-game

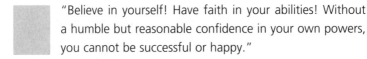

"Believe in yourself! Have faith in your abilities! Without a humble but reasonable confidence in your own powers, you cannot be successful or happy."

Norman Vincent Peale, minister and author

How Do You Want to Be Remembered?

You can often learn where you are going by looking backward. With hindsight, you can see where you might have made different choices leading to different outcomes. Thus, you learn not only from your successes but also from your mistakes. You are able to identify strengths as well as weaknesses. From this experience, you can move forward with awareness of your strengths and thus derive greater chance for success from this point forward.

This is a great advantage to those whose life stage brings them to a crossroads. No longer making choices in a tabula rasa, you have benefit of all the experience that has gone before. To make looking back productive and fruitful, learning must take place. You might spend some time in introspection, considering how your successes were shaped by the choices you made that leveraged your strengths. Perhaps you made choices that were inconsistent with your strengths. Finally, this reflection may give you self-confidence.

A useful exercise for looking backward to gain perspective for your future is to create your own eulogy. For what do you want to be remembered?

 "I want freedom for the full expression of my personality."

Mahatma Ghandi, political leader

Eulogy

Imagine that you lived a full life to the age of 90. What will your obituary say about you and the life you led? Complete the blank lines below:

Mr./Ms. _____, age 90, died on Saturday as a result of a brief illness. People who knew him/her best describe him/her as

_____, _____,

and _____.

He/She was employed by _____
_____ for _____ years.
During his/her lifetime, he/she accomplished _____
_____
_____
_____. He/she will be remembered most for
_____
_____.

He/she will be missed most especially by _____
_____
_____.

Your Life Roles

As an adult, you fill many roles such as worker, spouse, parent, boss, child, grandchild, and student. Your life requires that you give all of these roles attention and energy, sometimes to the point of exhaustion or sacrifice of one or some for others. By spending time learning who you are and what situations evoke your best self, you can minimize the disruption and collision of roles and instead provide a foundation and a bolstering of all roles by honoring your strengths.

"Opportunity is missed by most people because it is dressed in overalls and looks like work."

Thomas A. Edison, inventor

It is best for you to give your role of individual your undivided attention as often as you can. By providing yourself with the space and time that you need, you can better leverage the other roles with you as the foundation and pivot point.

Neglecting or denying the role of self creates role confusion in the other aspects of who you are. Take a few moments to jot down all of the roles that you play and how you are at your best in each role.

Spouse

_____

_____

_____

_____

Parent

_____

_____

_____

_____

Child

_____

_____

_____

_____

Neighbor

_____

_____

_____

_____

Worker

_____

_____

_____

_____

Boss

_____

_____

_____

_____

Student

_____

_____

_____

_____

Other _____

_____

_____

_____

Other _____

_____

_____

_____

Organizational Fit and Corporate Culture

A large part of a federal agency is its culture, that is, the environment within which employees interact and perform. An agency or department's culture can be viewed as its personality. Is it informal, with lines of authority blurred and ill-defined? Or is it bureaucratic, with a clear hierarchy of authority and governance? Organizational fit for who you are and what you envision for yourself is determined in large part by the culture of an organization.

Spend a few moments thinking about what type of agency is a good match for you. For example, is it large or small? Is it formal or informal?

_____

_____

_____

_____

Occupational Wellness

Many times individuals fall into jobs where they don't belong. They can find themselves trapped if they don't take action to move into other areas. This chapter provided you with some tools to focus the direction of your internal yearnings, strengths, and interests so that you are positioned to choose a federal career with awareness and direction.

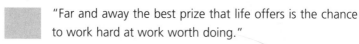

"Far and away the best prize that life offers is the chance to work hard at work worth doing."

Theodore Roosevelt, president

Throughout your career, it is important to take stock of where you are and to ask yourself if you are moving in a direction of your own choosing. It's never too late to get unstuck. Feel free to revisit this chapter and complete the exercises, with tabula rasa, each time your career feels at a standstill.

Closing Thoughts

This is not the time for you to question your motives, doubt your feelings, or consider your goals in the context of job opportunities or salary. Rather, consider it your opportunity to let your dreams and aspirations soar. Reality will come soon enough, when you move into the research and exploration phase of federal career planning. Right now you can be content to enjoy the ride of envisioning your highest self—that self who knows no bounds or limitations, who seeks challenges and opportunities just because they are there.

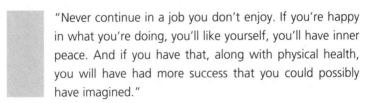

"Never continue in a job you don't enjoy. If you're happy in what you're doing, you'll like yourself, you'll have inner peace. And if you have that, along with physical health, you will have had more success that you could possibly have imagined."

Johnny Carson, comedian

This is an exciting journey that will create the foundation for the rest of your life. Take it seriously as well as the time to do it well.

CHAPTER 4

DEVELOPING YOUR CAREER IDENTITY

Rather than focus solely on work as a way to make a living, pay the bills, and provide for your family — which of course is important — you need to determine how work fits into your life as an integral aspect of who you are and what contribution you can make to the world.

This chapter helps you develop your federal career identity and a vision of your career, including the reasons you work, what you bring to the work, and how you can market your skills in the context of work.

Why Do You Work?

People work for a variety of reasons: income, personal satisfaction, and social interaction, among others. Research conducted by Frederick Herzberg (1923–2000) indicates that people are motivated to work by numerous and individual factors. Considered the pioneer of job enrichment, Herzberg and his colleagues wrote *The Motivation to Work,* which explores theories about workplace motivation.

Everyone has unique motivations and reasons for working, as well as factors for what makes work meaningful. To tap into your own motivation, you may wish to explore your own reasons for working, above and beyond the need to earn an income.

44

Take a few moments to complete the following statements.

I want a career that

_____

_____

_____

_____

_____

My skills and talents that make me uniquely qualified for such
a career include

_____

_____

_____

_____

_____

"Work is love made visible."

Kahlil Gibran, artist, poet, and writer

What Is Meaningful Work for You?

The vision you have of yourself for work is important to
consider when you explore how work can be meaningful for
you. Work is an extension of your place in the world, and

ideally it expresses who you are. In this section, you will explore the role that work plays in your life.

Consider that your work is led by what might be termed *your calling.* The word *vocation* has at its root the Latin word *vocare,* meaning *to call.* Often thought to apply only to religious work, the word can have broader application to anyone who has embarked on a search for work that is meaningful, contributes to the greater good, and has purpose beyond the immediate reward of salary.

A vocation is long-lasting and can survive the unpleasantness of the daily tasks that often comprise a job. A vocation encompasses the larger context within which a job, and even a career, can fit. In fact, a vocation provides meaning, keeps you moving forward, and will maintain your connection to work in a sustainable fashion. In short, it makes the tasks associated with the endeavor truly *your* work.

"Everyone has his own specific vocation or mission in life; everyone must carry out a concrete assignment that demands fulfillment. Therein he cannot be replaced, nor can his life be repeated, thus, everyone's task is unique as his specific opportunity to implement it."

Viktor E. Frankl, doctor, Holocaust survivor, and author

Jobs can come and go, based on the need of a society or an organization. Vocations, however, are sustaining, are rooted in one's purpose and sense of self, and are secured to the goals of the larger society.

Can you identify what you are called to do in life? Usually characterized by a passion or a great yearning to pursue a field, discipline, or venture, meaningful work and activities can sometimes make themselves known to you before you are aware of or identify them. Write your thoughts about your calling:

_____

_____

_____

_____

_____

Creating a Personal Mission Statement

An integral part of your career identity is a personal mission statement that encompasses the things that motivate you, your priorities, and your intent for work. A mission statement articulates your values and your purpose and identifies the factors that move you in a certain direction. Author Steven Covey identifies a mission statement as "connecting with your own unique purpose and the profound satisfaction that comes from fulfilling it."

By taking the time to write your mission statement, you excavate the elements that constitute your uniqueness and place them within a larger context of who you are. Invest in yourself and figure out what is most important to you. A mission statement can be the most important component of capturing your fundamental nature, building your brand, and creating your career. Developing a mission statement that identifies the core of who you are can provide a firm foundation for planning your federal career.

Here are mission statement examples:

"To live life creatively and help others achieve their creative purpose through dedication to the potential of human resources throughout the federal government."

"By using my knowledge of epidemiology and current health-care technologies, foster wellness and prosperity of all citizens through the development of health-care policy."

To begin writing your mission statement, complete the following statements.

What do you consider to be your best characteristics?

_____

_____

_____

_____

_____

How you do you reveal these characteristics to others?

_____

_____

_____

_____

What are some ways in which you would like to utilize these characteristics in your life and your work?

_____

_____

_____

_____

_____

"If you don't set your goals based upon your mission statement, you may be climbing the ladder of success only to realize, when you get to the top, you're on the wrong building."

Stephen Covey, author

Utilizing the information you gathered about yourself above, begin to craft your mission statement by completing the worksheet that follows.

My Personal Mission Statement

"I envision myself involved in activities that

_____

_____

_____

"For the purpose of _____

_____

_____

"With the following organizations/audiences:

_____

_____

_____ "

If there is anything else that you think is important enough to include in your mission statement, add it here:

_____

_____

_____

Now, put it all together to complete your mission statement:

_____

_____

_____

_____

_____

A mission statement is an organic, dynamic tool that evolves and grows over time as your experiences and credentials change. Don't make the mistake of writing your mission statement and then putting it away, never to be seen again. Keep it in plain view and refer to it often to ensure that you are living your life and pursuing your work in a purposeful way.

Later in the book, you will have the opportunity to match your mission statement with the mission and goals of federal departments and agencies, thus creating increased opportunity for consistency and integration between who you are, what you do, and where you perform the work. An agency's mission statement is a statement of purpose, defining why it exists and what it intends to accomplish.

Finding the career that is the best fit requires that you discover an agency that will allow you to work and perform genuinely and authentically. Being who you are, connecting with your purpose and your passion, is best accomplished in an agency whose values mirror your own. Find the right job with the right organization by matching your values and mission with an organization's values and mission. When your beliefs are consistent with an organization's belief system, you are in synchronicity and harmony with its purpose.

Identifying Your Life Purpose

Discovering your purpose is another aspect of your career identity and conveys the meaning in your life, which drives your actions. This drive guides you and provides a framework for who you are and what you do.

Considering your life purpose can provide a jump start to identifying a federal career. By exploring the essence of yourself as an individual with unique talents, you can discern an all-encompassing view of a career enhanced and infused by that which is uniquely you. Therefore, the federal career of your choosing is only possible when performed by you, with your unique perspective. Identify what energizes you, embodies who you are, and provides the substance to unearth your life purpose.

"Being busy does not always mean real work. The object of all work is production or accomplishment and to either of these ends there must be forethought, system, planning, intelligence, and honest purpose, as well as perspiration. Seeming to do is not doing."

Thomas A. Edison, inventor

Consider what you believe is the primary reason for your existence, what purpose you are here to serve, and what provides you with a deep sense accomplishment. You may begin by considering areas of your life from which you receive true satisfaction and a sense of fulfillment. Philosophically stated: What is the meaning of your life?

_____

_____

_____

_____

Developing a Personal Brand

Choosing between different items on a shelf in a grocery store is often a matter of making a choice between competing brands. The brand you consistently choose offers and delivers the promise of consistency, quality, value, or whatever qualities are inherent in the brand. Similarly, your talents, reputation, image, and other factors that encompass you constitute your brand.

A personal brand includes your reputation and the impression others have of you. A brand reflects who you are and shows through your actions what you stand for. You create and reinforce your personal brand. In everything you say and do, your brand is apparent.

You are your own brand manager, and you can influence how others react when they hear your name. A personal brand is authentic and organic and emanates from who you are in reality. It is not contrived, forced, or created, yet it must be cultivated, reinforced, and nurtured. In short, a personal brand is the image others have of you, in your absence.

Outer Image

What image do you convey? Do you know what others think of you? You may wish to ask a few colleagues or friends to provide you with an honest appraisal.

_____

_____

_____

_____

_____

Inner Image

Now, think about how you *want* to be perceived. What is the impression you wish to make? What is the brand identity you want to create?

_____

_____

_____

_____

_____

Comparing Your Inner and Outer Images

By comparing the two images (outer and inner), you have conducted a gap analysis. The difference between what others say about you and what you want them to see is the opportunity for development of your brand.

In the space below, examine how you can reconcile the difference between the image you convey with how you desire to be perceived.

_____

_____

_____

_____

 "The way to find out about your happiness is to keep your mind on those moments when you feel most happy, when you are really happy—not excited, not just thrilled, but deeply happy."

Joseph Campbell, mythologist, writer, and lecturer

Creating an Elevator Speech

An elevator speech, thus called because it can be delivered in the time it takes to ride an elevator, is a personal branding statement that informs the listener of your unique qualities and how these qualities can help the listener and his or her department or agency.

Sometimes called a personal pitch, creating this statement is important to help you define who you are, what you can do, and how you add value. You will use it while networking, in interviews, and any time you wish to convey your professional capability to an audience with the power and the connections to assist you in achieving your goals.

To create your elevator speech, begin with a short list of your most compelling qualities.

Descriptive adjectives that define you:

1. _____

2. _____

3. _____

Motivated skills from chapter 3:

1. _____

2. _____

3. _____

Now, put this information into an elevator speech by following the four steps described next.

Step 1: Focus on a Unique Self-Description

As you develop this description, consider what you want to remain in the listener's recollection of you. Include your name as the beginning of the introduction. This is the "who" of your introduction.

Example: *My name is Katy Hill. I am a marketing specialist with a variety of work experiences.*

Your turn:

_____

_____

_____

_____

_____

Step 2: Describe What You Do

This description should help the listener understand how you would add value. This is the "what" of your introduction. Refer to your list of descriptive adjectives.

Example: *I am creative, organized, and really enjoy brainstorming new ideas.*

Your turn:

_____

_____

_____

Step 3: Explain How You Are Unique

Explain how what you do is different or better than what others do. This is "how" you add value as part of your introduction.

Example: *People have told me that they've never met anyone who is as passionate about communicating information in new ways as I am.*

Your turn:

_____

_____

_____

Step 4: Describe Your Goal

In describing you goal, refer to your list of motivated skills. Also, it should be apparent to the listener what you are asking of him or her. This is the "what" from the listener's point of view, involving what he or she can do to help you achieve your goal.

Assembling a cohesive elevator speech communicates who you are and what you have to offer.

Example: *Right now, I'm looking for a federal job in a health-care setting, where I can be part of an environment that helps people. Here are two of my business cards. I'd appreciate it if you remember me when you hear of an opportunity for someone who loves creative communications.*

Your elevator speech:

_____

_____

_____

_____

_____

_____

_____

_____

_____

_____

Practice your speech until it sounds natural, not rehearsed. Use it whenever you need to sell yourself and your capabilities.

 "Whenever it is in any way possible, every boy and girl should choose as his life work some occupation which he should like to do anyhow, even if he did not need the money."

William Lyon Phelps, author, critic, and scholar

Developing Your Career Goal

Creating your career goal is a constructive process that evolves from all the work and answers you have provided in this chapter. How can your life purpose, mission statement, personal brand, and meaningful work combine into a career goal that satisfies all of the aspects of who you are and what is best for you? Your responses can lead to your ideal federal career.

With honest self-appraisal, you can create a career that is true to you, maximizes your skills and talents, focuses on your future, and contributes to the betterment of the world. When you consider that most of your waking hours are spent at your job, how do you envision spending your day? You can determine and choose what you are doing each and every day.

When you express yourself through your work, you are making art with your skills, talents, and personality. The artistry of your life can be self-evident through your work.

Spend enough time developing a career goal that articulates who you are. Develop an authentic response that you are proud of when people inquire about what you do. Your career goal will reflect who you are and how you want to spend your time.

In your career goal, you envision yourself engaged in activities that embody your authentic self and that flow from you without effort or thought. Tasks are effortless because they are part of you, yet they are also challenging. You tap into the innermost core of self, capitalizing on the qualities that drive your spirit and give your soul flight. You are unstoppable, because you're fueled by your own energy. You are self-directed. Your job is truly your life's work. You were destined for this work. All of your life, at some level, you dreamed of being in this job.

When people ask what you do, they gain an impression of who you are. You and your work are inextricably linked. When you have found work that reflects who you are, there is no separation between you and it. The connection is seamless, and your personal and professional identities are linked.

Spend a few minutes and create a vision of your career, including the reasons you work, what you bring to the work, and how you can market your skills in the context of work. You can refer back to the exercises you completed in chapter 3 to guide your responses.

Still, do not worry about what federal job you will seek or for which federal agency you will work. Only develop the vision of what you want.

My Vision of Work

My top three values:

_____

_____

_____

My top three motivated skills:

_____

_____

_____

(continued)

(continued)

The top three activities that I enjoy:

_____

_____

_____

Where I do/have done these activities:

_____

_____

_____

My audience (clients, population, students, and so on):

_____

_____

_____

My top three most significant accomplishments:

_____

_____

_____

I am (three descriptor words):

_____

_____

_____

I have expertise in these three areas:

_____

_____

_____

My top three strengths include

_____

_____

_____

I truly enjoy my line of work, and I look forward to similar positions in which I can use my skills to

_____

_____

_____

_____ (my passion/what I enjoy doing).

Closing Thoughts

You will use the information in this chapter to point you in the direction of the right federal fit.

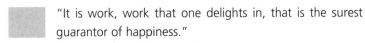

"It is work, work that one delights in, that is the surest guarantor of happiness."

Ashley Montague, author and anthropologist

PART III

BECOMING FAMILIAR WITH FEDERAL OPPORTUNITIES

Chapter 5: Introducing Federal Departments and Agencies and Federal Jobs

Chapter 6: Skills the Federal Government Is Seeking

Introducing Federal Departments and Agencies and Federal Jobs

This chapter introduces you to federal departments and agencies and to actual federal jobs so you can begin to consider the type of federal work that may suit you.

Federal Departments and What They Do

Most federal job opportunities are in the executive branch, which is comprised of departments designed to provide services, oversee programs, set policies, and improve the lives of U.S. citizens. These departments' myriad responsibilities require thousands of skilled professionals working in offices nationwide. The executive branch includes 15 cabinet departments detailed here. For more details, see the source of this list at http://www.makingthedifference.org/federalcareers/cabinetdepartments.shtml

In the past year, the top five federal hiring agencies for civil service jobs were Veterans Affairs (Veterans Health

Administration), Army (Corps of Engineers), Agriculture (Forest Service), Army (Medical Command), and Air Force.

U.S. Department of Agriculture (USDA)

The Agriculture Department has a broad range of responsibilities that include farming and agricultural products, food stamps and anti-poverty programs, and conservation and natural resource protection. Agriculture Department inspectors are responsible for the safety of the nation's food supply, and USDA employees run an array of rural development programs. The U.S. Forest Service, with its park rangers and firefighters, is a USDA agency.

U.S. Department of Commerce

The Commerce Department is in one way or another responsible for everything we buy and sell. Commerce officials regulate everything from foreign trade to fishing to the granting of patents. The department also oversees programs that support minority businesses and provides statistics and analyses for business and government planners. It forecasts the weather, charts the oceans, regulates patents and trademarks, conducts the census, and compiles economic statistics.

U.S. Department of Defense (DOD)

You don't have to enlist to be part of the nation's defense forces. The nearly 700,000 civilians working in the Defense Department are responsible for supplying military hardware, administering personnel pay and benefits, providing information to the public and military, managing military education programs, and attempting to locate missing personnel or prisoners of war. DOD manages the military forces that protect our country and its interests. Defense includes the departments of the Army, Navy, and Air Force and a number of smaller agencies.

U.S. Department of Education

The Education Department's first responsibility is making sure that the nation's public school systems provide students with proper school supplies, educational facilities, and qualified teachers. Department personnel promote parental involvement in their children's education, develop financial aid policies, and encourage the use of modern technology in the classroom. It monitors and distributes financial aid to schools and students, collects and disseminates data on schools and other educational matters, and prohibits discrimination in schools.

U.S. Department of Energy (DOE)

The Energy Department works to ensure that the nation has a steady, consistent, and safe supply of energy. Energy scientists work to harness the sun's power while its physicists attempt to capture nuclear energy for civilian or military use. It oversees the production and disposal of nuclear weapons and plans for future energy needs.

U.S. Department of Health and Human Services (HHS)

The Health and Human Services Department is the government's primary agency for overseeing the health and well-being of the American people. HHS employees work on more than 300 programs and perform essential services ranging from food safety to medical research to drug abuse prevention. It administers Medicare, Medicaid, and numerous other social service programs. HHS has regional offices across the country.

U.S. Department of Homeland Security (DHS)

The Homeland Security Department's first priority is to protect the nation against terrorist attacks. Component agencies analyze threats and intelligence, guard the nation's borders and airports, protect critical national infrastructure, and coordinate the nation's response for emergencies. It works to minimize the damage from attacks and natural disasters. It also administers the country's immigration policies and oversees the Coast Guard.

U.S. Department of Housing and Urban Development (HUD)

Housing and Urban Development Department personnel are responsible for ensuring that American families have access to decent, safe, and affordable housing. Among HUD's biggest programs are insuring mortgages for homes and loans for home improvement, making direct loans for construction or rehabilitation of housing projects for the elderly and the handicapped, providing federal housing subsidies for low- and moderate-income families, and enforcing fair housing and equal housing access laws.

U.S. Department of the Interior (DOI)

The Interior Department manages the nation's natural resources, from land and water to coal and natural gas.

By monitoring the extraction of natural resources, Interior Department personnel work to efficiently protect and preserve the environment. The department also houses the office responsible for overseeing Native American affairs. It manages federal lands (including the national parks) and runs hydroelectric power systems.

U.S. Department of Justice (DOJ)

Headed by the Attorney General, the Justice Department makes sure that federal laws aimed at protecting the public and promoting competitive business practices are implemented, including immigration and naturalization statutes, consumer safeguards, and criminal prosecutions. The FBI falls under the Justice Department's authority. It also works with state and local governments and other agencies to prevent and control crime. It enforces federal laws, prosecutes cases in federal courts, and runs federal prisons.

U.S. Department of Labor (DOL)

The Labor Department administers and enforces laws and regulations that ensure safe working conditions, minimum hourly pay, and overtime. Through its varied initiatives, it also works to meet the special employment-related needs of the disabled, the elderly, and minorities and provides job banks, unemployment benefits, and workplace health regulations. It regulates pension funds and collects and analyzes economic data.

U.S. Department of State

The State Department is responsible for the conduct of the nation's foreign affairs and diplomatic initiatives. State Department personnel coordinate conferences with foreign leaders, hammer out treaties and other agreements with foreign governments, and protect the safety of U.S. citizens traveling abroad. It oversees U.S. embassies and consulates, issues passports, monitors U.S. interests abroad, and represents the U.S. before international organizations.

U.S. Department of Transportation (DOT)

Cars, trucks, buses, trains, boats, and airplanes all fall under the Department of Transportation's authority. So does the nation's transportation infrastructure. The work of Transportation Department employees makes it possible for Americans to travel home for the holidays, away on vacation, and even to and from work. The Transportation Department is also home to the Transportation Security Administration, which is responsible for protecting the country's transportation systems and ensuring the safety of its passengers. The department sets national transportation policy and plans and funds the construction of highways and mass transit systems.

U.S. Department of the Treasury

Just look at the $20 bill in your wallet if you want to know what the Treasury Department does. Printing the nation's money is only one of many responsibilities overseen by the nation's second oldest cabinet department (only the State Department has been around longer). It also sets domestic financial, economic, and tax policy; manages the public debt; regulates banks and other financial institutions; and collects taxes. Less obvious is Treasury's other major role—law enforcement; the Secret Service and the Customs Service are Treasury agencies.

U.S. Department of Veterans Affairs (VA)

If you have served your country in the military, the Veterans Affairs Department is there to serve you. Best known for its health-care system, the VA also provides social support services, administers pensions and other veterans' benefits, and promotes the hiring of veterans. It also operates national cemeteries.

Key Federal Agencies and What They Do

While you'll find the majority of federal jobs in the cabinet departments, a number of very interesting and varied civil service opportunities exist at independent agencies, in government corporations, and in the Executive Office of the President.

Well-known independent agencies include the Federal Communications Commission, Office of Management and Budget, Peace Corps, and Securities and Exchange Commission. Although the majority of the agencies are small, employing fewer than 1,000 workers (many employ fewer than 100), some are quite large.

Following are descriptions of what some of the larger agencies do. For more details, see the source of this list at www. makingthedifference.org/federalcareers/federalagencies.shtml.

Congressional Budget Office (CBO)

The Congressional Budget Office provides Congress with nonpartisan analyses for economic and budgetary decisions. In addition to helping the congressional budget committees with economic forecasts and cost estimates for policies introduced in bills, the CBO also analyzes the president's budget.

Corporation for National and Community Service

Working with nonprofit and faith-based organizations, schools, and other entities, the Corporation for National and Community Service supports voluntary service of Americans of all ages through AmeriCorps, Senior Corps, and Learn and Serve.

Defense Applicant Assistance Office (DAAO)

The DAAO helps to connect Defense recruiters to potential applicants to provide the consistent contact and personalized service that can make the application process easier and transparent.

Environmental Protection Agency (EPA)

The EPA safeguards the nation's air, water, and land. Working with other federal agencies and state and local governments and Indian tribes, EPA employees are responsible for environmental research and standards setting.

Equal Employment Opportunity Commission (EEOC)

The EEOC enforces federal laws related to equal employment opportunity, including discrimination based on race, religion, national origin, gender, age, and disability.

Export-Import Bank of the United States (Ex-Im Bank)

The Ex-Im Bank helps U.S. exporters by providing guarantees of working capital loans and loan repayment plans to foreign purchasers of American goods.

Federal Communications Commission (FCC)

The FCC regulates interstate and international radio, television, satellite, cable, and wire communications.

Federal Deposit Insurance Corporation (FDIC)

The FDIC is the nation's insurer of bank deposits and is tasked with maintaining the stability of the nation's financial system.

Federal Emergency Management Agency (FEMA)

FEMA is the federal government's emergency preparedness and disaster response and relief entity. The scope of FEMA's work includes everything from floods to earthquakes to the transport of hazardous substances.

Federal Energy Regulatory Commission (FERC)

The FERC is an independent regulatory agency that regulates and oversees various aspects of the energy markets in the

United States. FERC's team of professional and technical specialists solves the problems of today's energy markets and sets policy direction for the energy industry at large.

Federal Reserve System

The Federal Reserve is the nation's central bank. It establishes monetary policy, supervises banking institutions, maintains the stability of the financial system, and provides financial services to the government as well as to the public and other institutions.

Government Accountability Office (GAO)

The GAO is the government's central watchdog agency. At the request of members of Congress, GAO personnel investigate, audit, and evaluate government programs and then issue public reports on their findings. These findings often help guide congressional and presidential policy decisions.

General Services Administration (GSA)

The GSA is the government's property manager, landlord, acquisitions specialist, and office supplier. The agency sets policy to ensure government money is being spent wisely and that government workplaces are up to date.

Library of Congress

The Library of Congress is the nation's library and serves as the research arm for Congress. It also has the distinction of being the largest library in the world, with more than 120 million books, recordings, maps, manuscripts, and photographs. The Congressional Research Service, part of the Library of Congress, provides nonpartisan research and analysis on any topic that a member or committee of Congress may want to understand better for policy development.

National Aeronautics and Space Administration (NASA)

NASA staff and astronauts are the nation's vanguards in space exploration. The Apollo missions and Space Shuttle flights are famous examples of NASA's work. NASA oversees aviation research and conducts exploration and research beyond the earth's atmosphere.

Nuclear Regulatory Commission (NRC)

The NRC regulates the nation's civilian use of nuclear material to protect public health and safety. The three main areas of oversight are nuclear reactors; the handling of nuclear waste; and the use of nuclear materials in medicine, industry, and other settings.

Office of the Director of National Intelligence (ODNI)

The Office of the Director of National Intelligence oversees all 16 organizations that comprise the U.S. Intelligence Community (IC). The ODNI's goal is to effectively integrate foreign, military, and domestic intelligence in defense of the homeland and of United States interests abroad. The ODNI is led by the director of national intelligence, who oversees and directs the implementation of the National Intelligence Program and serves as the principal adviser to the president, the National Security Council, and the Homeland Security Council for intelligence matters related to the national security.

Office of Management and Budget (OMB)

The OMB is responsible for formulating the president's budget and coordinating the administration's procurement and financial management. In the process of budget development, the OMB also evaluates and shapes agency programs and policies.

Office of Personnel Management (OPM)

OPM is the federal government's human resources agency. In addition to working with agencies to create systems to recruit, develop, manage, and retain a high quality and diverse workforce, OPM is also responsible for regulating these systems.

Securities and Exchange Commission (SEC)

The SEC's mission is to maintain the integrity of the nation's securities markets. It requires publicly held companies to report financial information so investors have the information they need to make investment decisions.

Social Security Administration

The Social Security Administration sends Social Security checks to the nation's retired and disabled and their families. It collects funds for these and other programs from earnings identified by each American's Social Security number.

The Smithsonian Institution

The Smithsonian Institution provides the American public with educational programs and research as well as access to dozens of museums and the National Zoo.

United States Agency for International Development (USAID)

USAID promotes economic growth and development abroad in support of U.S. foreign policy. Working with foreign governments as well as business and nonprofit organizations, USAID operates health, democracy, agriculture, and conflict-prevention programs.

Learning About Federal Occupations

Several sources can help you get familiar with federal jobs, including their responsibilities, education and training, and skills needed. Use the resources described in this section to begin researching federal work that interests you.

Occupational Outlook Handbook

Every two years, the U.S. Department of Labor's Bureau of Labor Statistics publishes the *Occupational Outlook Handbook (OOH)*, which provides—free of charge—the following information on hundreds of occupations that often have federal counterparts:

- Training and education needed
- Earnings
- Expected job prospects
- What workers do on the job
- Working conditions

The *OOH* also gives job search tips, links to information about the job market in each state, and more. You can find the *OOH* online at www.bls.gov/oco/ or in print at libraries and in bookstores. A print version of the *OOH* with additional career information is available through JIST Publishing (www.jist.com).

*O*NET Online*

The Occupational Information Network (O*NET) is the nation's primary source of occupational information. The O*NET database contains information on hundreds of standardized and occupation-specific descriptors. The database is available to the public at no cost and is continually updated by surveying a broad range of workers from each occupation. The database provides the basis for career exploration tools for job seekers and students.

A vital component of the O*NET is O*NET OnLine, which is an interactive application for exploring and searching occupations. Visit it at http://online.onetcenter.org.

See appendix B for an example of an O*NET job summary report.

USAJOBS

USAJOBS is a great place to get familiar with federal job opportunities. Go to www.usajobs.gov and click on Browse Jobs.

Here are the federal job categories identified on USAJOBS Browse Jobs by Occupation:

- Accounting, Budget, and Finance
- Biological Sciences
- Business, Industry, and Procurement
- Education
- Engineering and Architecture
- Equipment, Facilities, and Services
- Human Resources
- Information Technology
- Information, Arts, and Public Affairs
- Inspection, Investigation, Enforcement, and Compliance
- Legal and Claims Examining
- Library and Archives
- Management, Administration, Clerical, and Office Services
- Mathematics and Statistics
- Medical, Dental, and Public Health
- Physical Sciences
- Quality Assurance and Grading
- Safety, Health, and Physical and Resource Protection
- Social Science, Psychology, and Welfare

- Supply
- Trades and Labor
- Transportation
- Veterinary Medical Science

Through the Advanced Search and International Search options on USAJOBS, you can identify about 100 job titles. The Jobs in Demand search reveals a short list of high-paying specialized jobs that tend to fall into the science, technology, engineering, and mathematics (STEM) category.

A final method for getting familiar with federal occupations is to go to the USAJOBS Info Center's Accessible Version link. Click on Federal Jobs by College Major. Find your college major (no matter how old your degree) and review related jobs.

 "Desire ignites the fire, but someone still has to provide the fuel, fan the fire, and contain the flames."

Colin Ross Parker, artist

As you can see, the federal government offers a wide variety of occupations. When you are ready to begin your federal job search, you can use Search Jobs, Advanced Search, and International Search to see current openings in your field or area of interest and where they are located.

Top Fields Where Government Is Hiring

The Partnership for Public Service, www.ourpublicservice. org, is a nonprofit, nonpartisan organization that works to revitalize the federal government by inspiring a new generation to serve and by transforming the way government works.

Based on its 2009 survey of federal hiring managers, the partnership projects that hiring for mission-critical federal jobs will jump by more than 40 percent through fiscal 2010–2012 compared to the three previous years. *Mission-critical* can be defined as jobs that support the agency's mission statement. Mission statements are typically located on each agency's About Us web page.

By the end of September 2012, federal agencies will hire more than 270,000 workers. The partnership predicts that the three top-hiring federal agencies through fiscal year 2012 will be the Department of Homeland Security, Department of Veterans Affairs, and Department of Defense. Most federal hiring will take place in the following five categories.

Medical and Public Health (54,114 Projected Hires)

Occupational areas and positions include

- Physician (all disciplines)
- Nursing
- Dietician/nutrition
- Occupational and rehabilitation therapy
- Radiology
- Pharmacy
- Industrial hygiene
- Consumer safety

Security and Protection (52,077 Projected Hires)

Occupational areas and positions include

- Intelligence analysis
- International relations
- Foreign affairs
- Security administration
- Transportation security officer
- Park ranger
- Correctional officer
- Police officer

Compliance and Enforcement (31,276 Projected Hires)

Occupational areas and positions include

- Inspector
- Investigator (including criminal)
- Customs and border patrol and protection
- Import specialist
- Customs inspection

Legal (23,596 Projected Hires)

Occupational areas and positions include

- Attorney
- Contact representative
- Paralegal

- Passport/visa examining
- Claims examining/assistance

Administration/Program Management (17,287 Projected Hires)

Occupational areas and positions include

- Human resources
- Equal employment opportunity
- Management/program analysis
- Telecommunications
- Various clerical support activities

Top 50 Federal Occupations with the Most Postings

One key to landing your perfect job is staying up to date on the latest federal hiring trends. On USAJOBS, OPM displays the top 50 federal occupations with the most job postings in the current calendar year. The list is cumulative through the past calendar month. Check it out at www.usajobs.gov/mostpopularjobs/index.asp.

Closing Points

Learning about the different agencies and the jobs available in each will help you to target your federal job search effectively. Identifying federal agencies and jobs with openings and the most hiring can provide you with a clear advantage in finding a federal occupation that's right for you.

CHAPTER 6

SKILLS THE FEDERAL GOVERNMENT IS SEEKING

The federal government seeks applicants who possess certain defined competencies. A competency is a cluster of skills and the ability to use them to perform a job. OPM defines a competency as "a measurable pattern of knowledge, skills, abilities, behaviors, and other characteristics that an individual needs to perform work roles or occupational functions successfully."

Competence is achieved through a variety of means, such as experience, education, training, and personal and professional development. Competencies take into account the entire person, not merely isolated skill sets.

Competencies tend to be either general or technical. General competencies reflect the cognitive and social capabilities (for example, problem solving and interpersonal skills) required for job performance in a variety of occupations. Technical competencies are more specific and are tailored to the particular knowledge and skill requirements necessary for a certain job. OPM has conducted a number of studies to identify competencies for many federal occupations.

Fundamental Competencies

Every federal agency advertises the competencies it is seeking in its employees. Vacancy announcements require that applicants address competencies in their resumes and essays. An analysis of common federal occupations reveals the following fundamental competencies, in addition to the other specific competencies sought by each agency.

Oral Communication

Expresses information (for example, ideas or facts) to individuals or groups effectively, taking into account the audience and nature of the information (for example, technical, sensitive, or controversial); makes clear and convincing oral presentations; listens to others, attends to nonverbal cues, and responds appropriately.

Writing

Recognizes or uses correct English grammar, punctuation, and spelling; communicates information (for example, facts, ideas, or messages) in a succinct and organized manner; produces written information, which may include technical material that is appropriate for the intended audience.

Interpersonal Skills

Shows understanding, friendliness, courtesy, tact, empathy, concern, and politeness to others; develops and maintains effective relationships with others; may include effectively dealing with individuals who are difficult, hostile, or distressed; relates well to people from varied backgrounds and different situations; is sensitive to cultural diversity, race, gender, disabilities, and other individual differences.

Customer Service

Works with clients and customers (that is, any individuals who use or receive the services or products that your work unit produces, including the general public, individuals who work in the agency, other agencies, or organizations outside the government) to assess their needs, provide information or assistance, resolve their problems, or satisfy their expectations; knows about available products and services; is committed to providing quality products and services.

Self-Management

Sets well-defined and realistic personal goals; displays a high level of initiative, effort, and commitment toward completing assignments in a timely manner; works with minimal supervision; is motivated to achieve; demonstrates responsible behavior.

Teamwork

Encourages and facilitates cooperation, pride, trust, and group identity; fosters commitment and team spirit; works with others to achieve common goals of an organization.

Executive Core Qualifications (ECQs)

OPM helps to ensure the government selects strong leaders by developing core qualifications used to test new career appointees to the Senior Executive Service (SES). Federal executives are expected to demonstrate competence in areas of expertise that are essential for leading and managing.

In 1997 OPM developed Executive Core Qualifications (ECQs) after extensive research on the attributes of successful executives in both the private and public sectors. OPM defines the ECQs as the "competencies needed to build a federal corporate culture that drives for results, serves customers, and builds successful teams and coalitions within and outside the organization."

The ECQs were revalidated and reissued with a few modifications in 2006. In their current form, they represent the best thinking of organizational psychologists, human resources professionals at OPM and other agencies, and senior executives themselves.

For more information, see the sources of this information at www.opm.gov/ses/recruitment/competencies.asp and http://opm.gov/ses/references/GuidetoSESQuals_2010.pdf.

The ECQs are as follows.

Leading Change

This core qualification involves the ability to bring about strategic change, both within and outside the organization, to meet organizational goals. Inherent to this ECQ is the ability to establish an organizational vision and to implement it in a continuously changing environment.

Competencies:

- **Creativity and Innovation.** Develops new insights into situations, questions conventional approaches, encourages new ideas and innovations, designs and implements new or cutting-edge programs/processes.

- **External Awareness.** Understands and keeps up to date on local, national, and international policies and

trends that affect the organization and shape stakeholders' views. Is aware of the organization's impact on the
external environment.

- **Flexibility.** Is open to change and new information.
  Rapidly adapts to new information, changing conditions,
  or unexpected obstacles.

- **Resilience.** Deals effectively with pressure. Remains
  optimistic and persistent, even under adversity.
  Recovers quickly from setbacks.

- **Strategic Thinking.** Formulates objectives and priorities
  and implements plans consistent with long-term interests
  of the organization in a global environment. Capitalizes
  on opportunities and manages risks.

- **Vision.** Takes a long-term view and builds a shared
  vision with others. Acts as a catalyst for organizational
  change. Influences others to translate vision into action.

Leading People

This core qualification involves the ability to lead people
toward meeting the organization's vision, mission, and goals.
Inherent to this ECQ is the ability to provide an inclusive
workplace that fosters the development of others, facilitates
cooperation and teamwork, and supports constructive
resolution of conflicts.

Competencies:

- **Conflict Management.** Encourages creative tension and
  differences of opinions. Anticipates and takes steps to
  prevent counterproductive confrontations. Manages and
  resolves conflicts and disagreements in a constructive
  manner.

- **Leveraging Diversity.** Fosters an inclusive workplace where diversity and individual differences are valued and leveraged to achieve the vision and mission of the organization.

- **Developing Others**. Develops the ability of others to perform and contribute to the organization by providing ongoing feedback and by providing opportunities to learn through formal and informal methods.

- **Team Building.** Inspires and fosters team commitment, spirit, pride, and trust. Facilitates cooperation and motivates team members to accomplish group goals.

Results Driven

This core qualification involves the ability to meet organizational goals and customer expectations. Inherent to this ECQ is the ability to make decisions that produce high-quality results by applying technical knowledge, analyzing problems, and calculating risks.

Competencies:

- **Accountability.** Holds self and others accountable for measurable high-quality, timely, and cost-effective results. Determines objectives, sets priorities, and delegates work. Accepts responsibility for mistakes. Complies with established control systems and rules.

- **Customer Service.** Anticipates and meets the needs of both internal and external customers. Delivers high-quality products and services. Is committed to continuous improvement.

- **Decisiveness.** Makes well-informed, effective, and timely decisions, even when data are limited or solutions produce unpleasant consequences. Perceives the impact and implications of decisions.

- **Entrepreneurship.** Positions the organization for future success by identifying new opportunities. Builds the organization by developing or improving products or services. Takes calculated risks to accomplish organizational objectives.

- **Problem Solving.** Identifies and analyzes problems, weighs relevance and accuracy of information, generates and evaluates solutions, makes recommendations.

- **Technical Credibility.** Understands and appropriately applies principles, procedures, requirements, regulations, and policies related to specialized expertise.

Business Acumen

This core qualification involves the ability to manage human, financial, and information resources strategically.

Competencies:

- **Financial Management.** Understands the organization's financial processes. Prepares, justifies, and administers the program budget. Oversees procurement and contracting to achieve desired results. Monitors expenditures and uses cost-benefit thinking to set priorities.

- **Human Capital Management.** Builds and manages the workforce based on organizational goals, budget considerations, and staffing needs. Ensures that employees are appropriately recruited, selected, appraised, and rewarded. Takes action to address performance problems. Manages a multi-sector workforce and a variety of work situations.

- **Technology Management.** Keeps up to date on technological developments. Makes effective use of technology to achieve results. Ensures access to and security of technology systems.

Building Coalitions

This core qualification involves the ability to build coalitions internally and with other federal agencies, state and local governments, nonprofit and private sector organizations, foreign governments, or international organizations to achieve common goals.

Competencies:

- **Partnering.** Develops networks and builds alliances. Collaborates across boundaries to build strategic relationships and achieve common goals.

- **Political Savvy.** Identifies the internal and external politics that impact the work of the organization. Perceives organizational and political reality and acts accordingly.

- **Influencing/Negotiating.** Persuades others, builds consensus through give and take, gains cooperation from others to obtain information and accomplish goals.

SES Fundamental Competencies

Fundamental competencies are the personal and professional attributes that are critical to successful performance in the SES. The fundamental competencies are the attributes that serve as the foundation for each of the ECQs. Experience and training that strengthen and demonstrate the competencies enhance a candidate's overall qualifications for the SES.

These competencies are the foundation for success in each of the ECQs:

- **Interpersonal Skills.** Treats others with courtesy, sensitivity, and respect. Considers and responds appropriately to the needs and feelings of different people in different situations.

- **Oral Communication.** Makes clear and convincing oral presentations. Listens effectively. Clarifies information.

- **Integrity/Honesty.** Behaves in an honest, fair, and ethical manner. Shows consistency in words and actions. Models high standards of ethics.

- **Written Communication.** Writes in a clear, concise, organized, and convincing manner for the intended audience.

- **Continual Learning.** Assesses and recognizes own strengths and weaknesses. Pursues self-development.

- **Public Service Motivation.** Shows a commitment to serve the public. Ensures that actions meet public needs. Aligns organizational objectives and practices with public interests.

Closing Points

Competencies are a set of skills an individual has acquired over time. A competency can be readily demonstrated at any given moment. The federal government seeks both professional and technical competencies—professional competencies are addressed in this chapter. Technical competencies are also required, but they are job specific and are addressed in job opportunity announcements.

PART IV

TRANSLATING YOU TO THE FEDERAL GOVERNMENT

CHAPTER 7

FINDING YOUR FIT IN THE FEDERAL GOVERNMENT

I
n this chapter, you will connect what you have learned about yourself, about your career desires, and about federal employment with opportunities in the federal government. You have established and laid the groundwork for meaningful employment, on your terms, with your ideals.

A Career with the Government: Not Just a Job

The variety of positions, departments, and agencies comprising the federal government increases the likelihood that you can find your right livelihood with Uncle Sam. A career can span decades. As discussed earlier, ideally, your career will encompass more than a paycheck, benefits, and a place to go each day. With career planning, proper guidance, and research, you can be poised to seek and secure work in an occupation and with an agency that matches your qualifications, values, skills, and interests.

Considering Your Values

The most logical place to begin your search for a federal job fit is with your values. Values are non-negotiable and are fundamental to personal well-being, affiliation, and sense of worth. They convey who you believe yourself to be, and they identify your priorities. Aligning your values to those of an agency is key to matching your sense of purpose with the agency's purpose. Being out of sync with the values of an agency can lead to frustration, exhaustion, mental depletion, and burnout.

List the top three values from chapter 3 that you consider crucial to your life and work.

My Values
1._____
2._____
3._____

Considering Your Life Purpose

Now you want to consider your life purpose. In looking back at chapter 4, you spent time reflecting on what gives your life meaning. You considered how important it is to pursue work consistent with your life purpose, so that you are living and working in alignment with your authentic self. You spent time thinking about what makes you uniquely you and what you have to offer. As part of this exploration, you conceived and wrote your life purpose.

"Whatever the mind of man can conceive and believe, it can achieve."

Napoleon Hill, author

In the space below, revisit that section in chapter 4 and copy the life purpose statement. You will have the opportunity to connect your life purpose to a job in the government, so that you are earning a living in accordance with your vision of yourself.

My Life Purpose
_____
_____
_____
_____
_____

Considering Your Mission Statement

As part of the connection between you and your work, consider your personal mission statement. It includes the work that so energizes you that you would perform it regardless of pay. Career exploration and a personal mission statement can lead you to work that is personally rewarding, gratifying, challenging, uplifting, and purposeful and utilizes your unique interests, skills, talents, and values.

In the space below, indicate the mission statement that you created in chapter 4.

My Personal Mission Statement

My mission is to _____

_____

For _____

_____

With _____

Reviewing Federal Values and Mission Statements

An organization's mission statement is a formal short written statement of its goals. Finding a job in a federal agency whose work values and mission mirror yours can provide you with satisfying opportunities.

Spend some time reviewing the departments and agencies described in chapter 5 and browsing agency websites to identify the agencies whose missions resonate with your own. The following website lists all federal departments and agencies and links to their websites: http://www.usa.gov/Agencies/Federal/All_Agencies/index.shtml

Review agency mission statements to ensure that the actions of each organization, its overall goals, and its sense of direction align with your own personal goals and values. Determine where you feel you can make a contribution using your skills, talents, and strengths.

Your career exploration earlier in the book will help you to identify federal agencies or departments that fall within your realm of interest and capabilities and will help you narrow your choices. Spend time thinking about how your own personal life mission might connect with the mission and goals of your top three agency selections. This is an important step, so don't rush through it.

Indicate the top three agencies whose missions resonate and converge with your mission statement:

1. _____

2. _____

3. _____

"'Know Thyself' was written over the portal of the antique world. Over the portal of the new world, 'Be Thyself' shall be written."

Oscar Wilde, writer

In the space below, write the mission statements of these agencies:

1. _____

_____

2. _____

_____

3. _____

_____

Connecting with an Agency's Mission and Strategic Plan

Consider what about the organizational missions resonates with you. Is it a focus on the environment? Do the organizations commit to the health and safety of vulnerable populations? Does a concentration on national security have meaning for you?

In the space below, describe the aspects of the agency missions that connect with you. Include how your own values and sense of purpose can be enhanced by being part of the organizations.

_____

_____

_____

_____

_____

_____

Included in this process should be a review of a department or agency's strategic plan. In a strategic plan, organizations identify where they want to be at a determined point in the future and how they plan to get there. Strategic planning involves attention to organizational changes, internally and externally, with a focus on how these trends affect the organization. Every government organization publishes its strategic plan.

Links to each agency's strategic plan can be found in our book, *Guide to America's Federal Jobs* (JIST Publishing), or by researching agency websites.

Review the strategic plans of the three organizations that interest you the most and summarize their strategic plans here:

1. _____

   _____

   _____

2. _____

   _____

   _____

3. _____

   _____

   _____

Considering Your Skills

Research shows that workers who are engaged in work that motivates them, as well as uses the skills they enjoy, experience greater career satisfaction. This satisfaction leads to greater work productivity, because workers constantly seek new opportunities to engage in work that they enjoy.

 "If all people knew of you was your work, would they know you?"

Willie Nelson, singer-songwriter

What could be better than to have the opportunity to use skills that you like and that are desired by a federal employer?

As indicated in chapter 3, some career experts estimate that the average American worker has approximately 700 skills.

When performed over a period of time, many of these skills can become drudgery, despite a person's ability to exercise them. A better way to translate skills to a job is to focus on motivated skills. Motivated skills are the skills you find interesting each time you use them. You enjoy using these skills so much that you are motivated to employ them on a regular basis. They are the unique personal characteristics that you must utilize in your work for you to maximize career satisfaction.

Employing Your Career Interests

Chapter 3 shares the six career themes of John Holland: realistic (hands on), investigative (problem solver), artistic (idea creator), social (people helper), enterprising (people influencer), and conventional (organizer). The top two or three themes to which you are instinctively attracted are your career interests. Career interests are made up of the skills you enjoy using the most. These, too, are your motivated skills.

Using the information you gathered in chapter 3, indicate your top three motivated skills and interests below.

My Motivated Skills/Interests

1._____

2._____

3._____

Matching Your Skills and Interests to Top 10 Federal Jobs

This section provides the most relevant information from postings of the top 10 federal occupations listed on USAJOBS (www.USAJOBS.gov). Using information you gained about yourself in chapters 3 and 4, you can determine whether your skills, interests, and other factors are a good match for these popular federal jobs.

By reviewing these jobs and thinking about your skills and interests, you will gain the ability to analyze federal vacancy announcements and determine whether the openings are a good fit for you.

It is critical that you study the qualifications and evaluation sections of each announcement to determine whether you meet the qualifications of the position. Do not make your decision on job title alone. Each federal department and agency has unique requirements for a job. Conduct an analysis of each announcement, paying particular attention to qualifications and evaluations to determine your fit for the position. Get comfortable studying vacancy announcements, and you will know what qualifications you must have as well as how your application will be evaluated.

"Sometimes you've got to let everything go—purge yourself. If you are unhappy with anything...whatever is bringing you down, get rid of it. Because you'll find that when you're free, your true creativity, your true self, comes out."

Tina Turner, singer

You will find that there is quite a bit of jargon as you work your way through the vacancy information. Chapter 10 provides specific help on how to read a vacancy announcement. It also covers the other sections of a vacancy announcement. Vacancy announcements have a total of five sections. A complete sample announcement appears in the appendix.

In the jobs that follow, you will see references to *KSAs*. KSAs refer to knowledge, skills, and abilities. Chapter 10 explains KSAs. You will also see references to *GS levels* in the jobs that follow. GS or *General Schedule* is the name for a pay scale utilized by the majority of white-collar personnel in the civil service of the federal government. GS is separated into 15 grades (GS-1, GS-2, and so on). Entry-level positions are generally in the GS-1 through GS-7 range. Grades GS-8 through GS-12 indicate a mid-level position. GS-13, GS-14, and GS-15 are reserved for top-level positions.

The areas in **bold** text are the position's specialized experience requirements, which you must have to be qualified for the job.

1. Information Technology Management Specialist

This position was posted with the Veterans Administration.

You can qualify by meeting either the educational or experience requirements.

QUALIFICATIONS REQUIRED:

Education: At the GS-5 level, a bachelor's degree. GS-7 or equivalent, one full year of graduate level education or superior academic achievement. GS-9 or equivalent, master's degree or equivalent level education or two full years of progressively higher level graduate education leading to a master's degree or equivalent graduate degree.

All academic degrees and coursework must be from accredited or pre-accredited institutions. Degrees must be computer science, engineering, information science, information systems management, mathematics, operations research, statistics, or technology management or degree that provided a minimum of 24 semester hours in one or more of the fields identified above and required the development or adaptation of applications, systems, or networks.

OR

Experience: Experience must be IT related; the experience may be demonstrated by paid or unpaid experience and/or completion of specific, intensive training (for example, IT certification) as appropriate. For all grade levels, individuals must demonstrate they have experience in the four competencies listed below:

1. Attention to Detail: Is thorough when performing work and conscientious about attending to detail.

2. Customer Service: Works with clients and customers (that is, any individuals who use or receive the services or products that your work unit produces, including general public, individuals who work in the agency, other agencies, or organizations outside the government) to assess their needs, provide information or assistance, resolve their problems, or satisfy their expectations; knows available products and services; is committed to providing quality products and services.

3. Oral Communication: Expresses information (for example, ideas or facts) to individuals or groups effectively, taking into account the audience and nature of the information (for example, technical, sensitive, controversial); makes clear and convincing oral presentations; listens to others, attends to nonverbal cues, and responds appropriately.

4. Problem Solving: Identifies problems, determines accuracy and relevance of information, uses sound judgment to generate and evaluate alternatives and to make recommendation.

AND

Specialized Experience for GS-7 (or equivalent) and Above: Positions at GS-7 (or equivalent) and above require one year of specialized experience at the next lower GS grade (or equivalent). **Specialized experience is experience that has equipped the applicant with the particular competencies/ knowledge, skills, and abilities to successfully perform the duties of the position and is typically in or related to the work of the position to be filled. Specialized experience would have been gained in positions that require knowledge of the installation of IT systems and information security principles. Experience would have also given the applicant the ability to apply these principles to troubleshoot and resolve system and software problems.**

You must be a U.S. citizen to qualify for this position.

You will need to successfully complete a background security investigation before you can be appointed into this position.

HOW YOU WILL BE EVALUATED:

In addition to the basic qualifications, the Knowledge, Skills, and Abilities (personal essays) below will be used to evaluate applicants. Applicants' responses to the KSAs will be the primary source document for evaluating qualifications and rating and ranking of candidates. Other documents (application, supervisory appraisal, performance appraisal, and applicable awards recognition, etc.) will also be used.

KSAs: Applicants are requested to complete VAF 5-4676a (Supplemental Qualification Statement) on plain bond paper addressing these basic knowledge, skills, abilities, and other characteristics (KSAs):

1. Experience in supporting Microsoft Operating System XP, XP Professional, and Microsoft Office products to include 2003 and 2007.

2. Knowledge of a wide range of IT diagnostic tools, principles, standards, and procedures to perform a variety of assignments in the assigned application or specialty area.

3. Experience in configuration, deployment, and support of desktop PC computer systems to include troubleshooting of both the PC system and peripheral equipment.

4. Knowledge of appropriate VA policies, operating procedures, and information flow and of prevailing IT practices in government agencies and the private sector sufficient to evaluate and recommend adoption of new or enhanced approaches to delivering IT services.

5. Ability to communicate effectively, both orally and in writing, to be able to influence various users in utilizing proper techniques and methods for efficient use of computer systems, as well as the ability to exchange and obtain necessary information.

2. Management and Program Analyst

This position was posted with the Veterans Administration.

QUALIFICATIONS REQUIRED:

Fifty-two weeks of specialized experience equivalent to the GS-11 grade level that equipped the applicant with the particular knowledge, skills, and abilities (KSAs) to perform successfully the duties of a Management and Program Analyst, a Management Analyst, or a Program Analyst. Qualifying experience is typically in or related to the position to be filled. **Specialized experience may have been gained performing work that involved analyzing and evaluating the effectiveness of programs and operations, that involved developing life cycle cost analyses of projects or performing cost benefit or economic evaluations of current or projected programs, or that involved other work related to management and program analysis.**

Qualifying experience may be obtained in the private or public sectors. Your qualifications will be evaluated on the following competencies (knowledge, skills, abilities, and other characteristics):

Knowledge, Skills and Abilities:

1. Knowledge of analytical and evaluative methods and techniques for assessing program development or execution and improving organizational effectiveness and efficiency.

2. Knowledge of management principles and processes.

3. Skill in application of fact finding and investigative techniques.

4. Ability to communicate orally and in writing.

5. Ability to develop presentations and reports.

Note: Some positions require an understanding of basic budgetary and financial management principles and techniques as they relate to long-range planning of programs and objectives.

Part-time or unpaid experience: Credit will be given for appropriate unpaid work on the same basis as for paid experience. Part-time experience will be credited on the basis of time actually spent in appropriate activities. To receive credit for such experience you must indicate clearly the nature of the duties and responsibilities in each position held and the number of hours per week spent in such employment.

HOW YOU WILL BE EVALUATED:

Basis of Rating: Once the application process is complete, a review of your application will be made to ensure you meet the job requirements. To determine if you are qualified for this job, a review of your resume and supporting documentation will be made. Please follow all instructions carefully.

3. Administration and Program Staff

This position was posted with the Veterans Administration.

QUALIFICATIONS REQUIRED:

Applicants can qualify by meeting the EDUCATION requirements specified and/or the SPECIALIZED EXPERIENCE requirements.

EDUCATION:

GS-7: Successful completion of one full year of progressively higher level graduate education leading to a degree in Management, Business Administration, or Public Administration.

OR

Superior Academic Achievement: To qualify based on superior academic achievement, you must have completed the requirements for a bachelor's degree from an accredited institution AND must meet certain GPA requirements.

GS-09: Successful completion of two full years of progressively higher level graduate education leading to a master's or equivalent graduate degree in Management, Business Administration, or Public Administration.

TRANSCRIPTS are required if

You are qualifying for this position based on education.

You are qualifying for this position based on a combination of experience and education.

You are qualifying for this position based on Superior Academic Achievement.

This education must have been successfully completed and obtained from an accredited school, college, or university.

SPECIALIZED EXPERIENCE AT THE GS-7/9 GRADE LEVELS:

Applicants must have one year of specialized experience equivalent in level of difficulty and responsibility to the next lower level in the federal service. This experience may have been obtained in the private or public (local, county, state, federal) sectors.

Examples of qualifying experience include but are not limited to

Designing, interpreting, and applying administrative policies, procedures, work processes, etc.

Auditing administrative processes (e.g., travel, time and attendance, budget, procurement, etc.).

Formulating and implementing travel budgets.

Developing procedures and systems for reporting and controlling travel budgets.

Performing technical writer-editor functions to ensure that correspondence meets standards for formatting, quality, and policy and procedures, and is appropriate for recipient.

Analyzing particular problem areas and making recommendations for improvements.

Performing research to collect information and develop technically sound responses for a general audience.

COMBINATION OF EDUCATION and EXPERIENCE AT THE GS-7/9 GRADE LEVELS:

Applicants may have combinations of successfully completed education and specialized experience to meet total qualification requirements. The total percentages must equal at least 100 percent to qualify an applicant for that grade level.

Special Conditions:

U.S. citizenship.

As a condition of employment, a background investigation may be required for this position.

HOW YOU WILL BE EVALUATED:

Your application will be rated on the extent and quality of your experience, education, and training relevant to the position. Your resume must support that you meet the specialized experience requirements described.

Your final rating will be based on your responses to the assessment questionnaire. Please ensure your resume provides enough detail to support your responses.

If, after reviewing your resume and/or supporting documentation, a determination is made that you have inflated your qualifications and/or experience, your score can/will be adjusted to more accurately reflect your abilities. Please follow all instructions carefully. Errors or omissions may affect your rating. Deliberate attempts to falsify information may be grounds for not selecting you.

4. Medical Officer

This position was posted at the Veterans Administration.

QUALIFICATIONS REQUIRED:

Qualification Standards Used: VA Handbook 5005, Part II, Appendix G2. These standards are available for review in the local HR Office.

Basic Requirements:

Citizenship. Citizen of the United States. (Noncitizens may be appointed when it is not possible to recruit qualified citizens in accordance with current regulations.)

Education. Degree of doctor of medicine or an equivalent degree resulting from a course of education in medicine or osteopathic medicine. The degree must have been obtained from one of the schools approved by the Secretary of Veterans Affairs for the year in which the course of study was completed.

Licensure and Registration. Current, full, and unrestricted license to practice medicine or surgery in a state, territory, or commonwealth of the United States or in the District of Columbia. The physician must maintain current registration in the state of licensure if this is a requirement for continuing active, current licensure.

Physical Standards. See VA Directive and Handbook 5019.

English Language Proficiency. Physicians, including residents, appointed to direct patient-care positions must be proficient in spoken and written English as required by 38 U.S.C. 7402(d) and 7407(d).

Grade Requirements: Not applicable.

You must submit to a drug test and receive a negative drug test before you can be appointed into this position.

You will need to successfully complete a background security investigation before you can be appointed into this position.

Applicants for this position must pass a pre-employment medical examination.

5. Nurse

This position was posted at the Veterans Administration.

QUALIFICATIONS REQUIRED:

You must possess a year of general work experience that shows your ability to perform progressively more complex, responsible, or difficult duties and that shows your ability to learn the specific work of this job.

To qualify based on education, submit copy of transcript or list of courses with credit hours, major(s), and grade-point average or class ranking. Application materials will not be returned. You can receive credit for education received outside the United States if you provide evidence that it is comparable to an accredited educational institution in the United States when you apply.

You must be a U.S. citizen to qualify for this position.

After appointment, you will be subject to random testing for illegal drug use.

You will need to successfully complete a background security investigation before you can be appointed into this position.

Applicants for this position must pass a pre-employment medical examination.

HOW YOU WILL BE EVALUATED:

You will be evaluated based on the question responses you provide during a structured interview. In responding to structured interview questions, you should be sure to cite specific examples of experience, explain exactly what you did, and the outcome.

6. Office Clerk/Assistant

This position was posted with the Veterans Administration.

QUALIFICATIONS REQUIRED:

Candidates must be citizens of the United States. One year of specialized experience equivalent to at least the GS-5 level. **Specialized experience is documented experience in clinic scheduling, tracking/ordering supplies, formatting memos and correspondence, using various software such as CPRS, Vista, Excel, Microsoft Word.** This position requires a qualified typist (40 WPM).

KNOWLEDGE, SKILLS AND ABILITIES TO BE ADDRESSED:

1. Telephone, oral, and written communication skills that enable incumbent to offer excellent service and resolve problems in a friendly manner with clinical and administrative staff, patients, families, and visitors.

2. Ability to follow routine administrative procedures with knowledge of clerical practices and office routine.

3. Ability to gather and compile data, including numerical data for reports, and the ability to apply basic analytical methods to various aspects of assigned program.

4. Knowledge of medical terminology.

5. Skill in operating a personal computer and related software, i.e., Word, Vista, CPRS, Excel, etc.

6. Ability to participate in performance improvement activities related to program quality and improvement processes.

Performance-based interviews may be conducted. If performance-based interviews are conducted, current employees are entitled to have a union observer. All applicants providing direct patient care services are required to demonstrate proficiency in spoken and written English as required by VA Handbook 5005, Part II, Appendix I. This agency provides reasonable accommodations to applicants with disabilities. If you need a reasonable accommodation for any part of the application and hiring process, please notify the agency. The decision on granting reasonable accommodation will be on a case-by-case basis.

Note: Failure to document qualifying typing (40 WPM) and office automation (OA) skills in your application material/official personnel folder prior to the closing date of this announcement may result in disqualification from this position.

You must be a U.S. citizen to qualify for this position.

After appointment, you will be subject to random testing for illegal drug use.

You will need to successfully complete a background security investigation before you can be appointed into this position.

You must be able to type at least 40 words per minute. You can self-certify by submitting a statement that you can type this speed.

Applicants for this position must pass a pre-employment medical examination.

HOW YOU WILL BE EVALUATED:

You will be evaluated to determine if you meet the minimum qualifications required and on the extent to which your application shows that you possess the knowledge, skills, and abilities associated with this position as defined next. When describing your knowledge, skills, and abilities, please be sure to give examples and explain how often you used these skills, the complexity of the knowledge you possessed, the level of the people you interacted with, the sensitivity of the issues you handled, etc.

1. Telephone, oral, and written communication skills that enable incumbent to offer excellent service and resolve problems in a friendly manner with clinical and administrative staff, patients, families, and visitors.

2. Ability to follow routine administrative procedures with knowledge of clerical practices and office routine.

3. Ability to gather and compile data, including numerical data for reports and the ability to apply basic analytical methods to various aspects of assigned program.

4. Knowledge of medical terminology.

5. Skill in operating a personal computer and related software, i.e., Word, Vista, CPRS, Excel, etc.

6. Ability to participate in performance improvement activities related to program quality and improvement processes.

7. Contract Specialist

This position was posted at NASA.

Qualifications Required:

Applicants must meet the basic education requirements for the GS-1102 series:

A. Four-year course of study leading to a bachelor's degree with a major in any field, or

B. At least 24 semester hours in any combination of the following fields: accounting, business, finance, law, contracts, purchasing, economics, industrial management, marketing, quantitative methods, or organization and management.

Exception: Employees who occupied GS-1102 positions on January 1, 2011, at grades 5 through 12 will be considered to meet the basic requirements for other GS-1102 positions up to and including the GS-12 level.

For advancement to the GS-13 level and above, applicants must show the following:

A. Completion of all mandatory agency training prescribed for progression to GS-13 and above and at least four years of experience in contracting or related positions AND

B. A four-year course of study leading to a bachelor's degree with a major in any field that includes or is supplemented by at least 24 semester hours in any combination of the following fields: accounting, business, finance, law, contracts, purchasing, economics, industrial management, marketing, quantitative methods, or organization and management.

Applicant must have one year of specialized experience equivalent to the next lower grade, which has equipped the applicant with the particular competencies needed to successfully perform the duties of the position described previously.

GS-12: Specialized experience is defined as experience in solicitation/contract development, including various contract types and methods to procure large equipment systems, programs, and services where little or no contractual precedent exists; experience with cost reimbursement contracting, including ability to assess financial management reports; experience to perform a broad range of contract administration functions with high-dollar and visible procurements with multiple years for significant programs.

GS-13: Specialized experience is defined as experience in solicitation/contract development, including various contract types and methods to procure large, highly complex, and significant equipment systems, programs, and services where little or no contractual precedent exists; experience with cost reimbursement contracting, including ability to assess financial management reports; experience to independently perform a broad range of contract administration functions with complex, high-dollar, and visible procurements with multiple years for significant programs.

HOW YOU WILL BE EVALUATED:

Resumes will be rated by an automated system (Resumix) that matches the competencies extracted from the candidate's resume to the competencies identified by the selecting official for the position. Candidates will be evaluated on the competencies they possess that are directly related to the duties of the job, as described in the announcement. Candidates should refer to NASA's Applicant Guide for assistance in developing a complete resume, as NASA will not accept separate KSA statements.

Qualified candidates will be assigned to one of three quality levels based on the degree to which their competencies meet the duties required. A human resources specialist will validate the qualifications of those candidates eligible to be referred to the selecting official. For the purpose of the Career Transition Assistance Program (CTAP) and the Interagency Career Transition Assistance Program (ICTAP), candidates rated in the top quality level are considered well-qualified.

8. Business and Industry Specialist

This position was posted for the Department of Defense.

QUALIFICATIONS REQUIRED:

DAWIA REQUIREMENTS: Employee must meet, or be capable of meeting, Defense Acquisition Workforce Improvement Act (DAWIA) requirements applicable to the duties of the position. Selectee must be able to complete DAWIA certification requirements within 24 months of placement into the position.

SPECIALIZED EXPERIENCE FOR GS-11 POSITIONS: Applicants must possess 52 weeks of specialized experience (equivalent to the GS-09 grade level) that equipped the applicant with the particular knowledge, skills, and abilities to perform successfully the duties of position and that is typically in or related to the work of the position.

SPECIALIZED EXPERIENCE FOR GS-12 POSITIONS: Applicants must possess 52 weeks of specialized experience (equivalent to the GS-11 grade level) that equipped the applicant with the particular knowledge, skills, and abilities to perform successfully the duties of position and that is typically in or related to the work of the position.

Qualifying experience may be obtained in the private or public sectors. Your qualifications will be evaluated on the following competencies (knowledge, skills, abilities, and other characteristics):

KNOWLEDGE, SKILLS, AND ABILITIES:

1. Knowledge of laws, principles, policies, and practices of systems acquisition and program management.

2. Knowledge of business, industrial management, contracting procedures, technical concepts, and production practices to evaluate contractor proposals and activities.

3. Knowledge of the missions, roles, functions, organizational structures, and operation of the Department of Defense, Air Force, and other entities that govern, interface with, and/or influence the systems acquisition process and integrated life cycle management.

4. Ability to plan, organize, and manage critical aspects of research, development, production, and support of subsystems or equipment and integrate, analyze, and manage a variety of acquisition functions and personnel in support of the process.

5. Ability to communicate both orally and in writing, clearly, concisely, and with technical accuracy.

Part-time or unpaid experience: Credit will be given for appropriate unpaid work on the same basis as for paid experience. Part-time experience will be credited on the basis of time actually spent in appropriate activities. To receive credit for such experience you must indicate clearly the nature of the duties and responsibilities in each position held and the number of hours per week spent in such employment.

You MUST provide transcripts to support your educational claims. Unless otherwise stated, unofficial transcripts on college letterhead are acceptable.

SPECIAL INSTRUCTIONS FOR FOREIGN EDUCATION: Education completed in foreign colleges or universities may be used to meet the requirements. You must show proof that the education credentials have been submitted to a private organization that specializes in interpretation of foreign educational credentials and that such education has been deemed to be at least equivalent to that gained in conventional U.S. education programs, or an accredited U.S. state university reports the other institution as one whose transcript is given full value, or full value is given in subject areas applicable to the curricula at the state university. It is your responsibility to provide such evidence when applying.

CONDITIONS OF EMPLOYMENT/OTHER SIGNIFICANT FACTS:

- The employee may be subject to random drug testing.

- Employee may be required to work overtime.

- Employee may be required to obtain and maintain appropriate certifications.

- The employee must meet the Defense Acquisition Workforce Improvement Act (DAWIA) requirements applicable to the duties of the position.

- The position has been designated as an acquisition position and is covered by the Acquisition Professional Development Program (APDP).

- The work requires the employee to occasionally travel away from the normal duty station via military or commercial aircraft.

- Employee is expected to meet Continuing Acquisition Education requirements.

HOW YOU WILL BE EVALUATED:

Basis of Rating: Once the application process is complete, a review of your application will be made to ensure you meet the job requirements. To determine if you are qualified for this job, a review of your resume and supporting documentation will be made. Please follow all instructions carefully.

NOTE: Applicants must submit transcripts if using education to qualify.

9. Engineer, General

This position was posted with the Nuclear Regulatory Commission.

QUALIFICATIONS REQUIRED:

To qualify for this position, you must have at least one year of specialized experience at the next lower grade level in the federal service or equivalent experience in the private or public sector. You must meet the qualifications for this position no later than 30 days after the date you submit your application and before placement in the position.

Bachelor's degree in the academic disciplines listed that shows a good knowledge of the theory, principles, and practices in the discipline (or an equivalent combination of education, training, and experience), PLUS three–five years of specialized experience in the specific occupation; OR one year of specialized experience at the next lower grade level OR equivalent in the specific occupation or a closely related occupation performing similar duties. **Specialized experience is defined as work experience applying any of these professional engineering and scientific disciplines:**

- Chemical Engineering
- Civil Engineering
- Electrical Engineering
- Electronic Engineering (Digital Instrumentation and Control)
- Environmental Science
- Fire Protection Engineering
- Geotechnical Engineering
- Geology
- Geophysics
- Health Physics
- Industrial Engineering (Human Factors)
- Materials Engineering
- Mechanical Engineering
- Metallurgical Engineering
- Nuclear Engineering
- Structural Engineering
- Chemistry
- Fire Safety Technology
- Hydrology

- Materials Science

- Metallurgy

- Nuclear Chemistry

- Nuclear Physics

- Physics

- Radiochemistry

- Radiological Science

- Seismology

- Welding

HOW YOU WILL BE EVALUATED:

Your application will be rated based on your responses to vacancy questions to determine your level of knowledge, skill, and ability related to the job requirements. Applications will be rated against the following criteria:

Experience related to Nuclear Reactors or

Experience related to Nuclear Power Plant Construction or

Experience related to Fuel Cycle or

Experience related to Nuclear Materials or

Experience related to Nuclear Waste or

Experience related to Risk Assessment or

Experience related to Technical Project Management AND

Ability to present technical information both orally and in writing.

10. Human Resources Specialist

This position posted with the Veterans Administration.

QUALIFICATIONS REQUIRED:

GS-11: One year of specialized experience equivalent to at least GS-9, or Ph.D. or equivalent doctoral degree, or three full years of progressively higher level graduate education leading to such a degree or LL.M. if related.

SPECIALIZED EXPERIENCE: Experience that equipped the applicant with the particular knowledge, skills, and abilities (KSAs) to perform successfully the duties of the position and that is typically in or related to the work of the position to be filled.

You must be a U.S. citizen to qualify for this position. You will need to demonstrate proficiency in writing, reading, and speaking English. You will need to successfully complete a background security investigation before you can be appointed into this position.

HOW YOU WILL BE EVALUATED:

You will be evaluated to determine if you meet the minimum qualifications required and on the extent to which your application shows that you possess the knowledge, skills, and abilities associated with this position. When describing your knowledge, skills, and abilities, please be sure to give examples and explain how often you used these skills, the complexity of the knowledge you possessed, the level of the people you interacted with, the sensitivity of the issues you handled, etc.

Please address all of the following rating factors:

1. Ability to maintain an assigned block of services, both Title 5 and Title 38, to ensure timely completion of all HR functions related to the block of assignment.

2. Ability to analyze organizational and operational problems and develop solutions.

3. Ability to efficiently and responsibly manage employee recruitment and retention for a large organization. Describe experience and accomplishments.

4. Ability to communicate orally and in writing (e.g., strong customer service skills, experience speaking in meetings or making presentations to groups, and experience in writing policy documents and preparing responses to inquiries from a variety of sources).

5. Ability to establish priorities and to adjust to and respond to changing issues, requirements, and situations.

Closing Thoughts

In chapter 3, you explored your values, skills, interests, and other important aspects of self-assessment. In chapter 4, you connected your self-exploration to a career goal. You may have wondered, is all of this possible in a federal job?

In this chapter, you matched yourself to federal departments and agencies with diverse missions and goals. You reviewed the qualifications and evaluation sections of top federal jobs to begin the process of identifying opportunities that suit you.

A career with the government can be as unique as you and the talents you bring to it!

CHAPTER 8

CLOSING YOUR SKILLS GAP

A fter reviewing federal jobs, you may determine that you do not possess the necessary skills or education to move in the direction of your goals. This chapter gives you the opportunity to explore resources to prepare you for your right livelihood. It helps you discover options for bridging possible education gaps, including obtaining career-related certifications in a cost- and time-effective manner.

A certification is a formal process of making certain that an individual is qualified in terms of particular knowledge or skills. Certification programs are often fostered by a certifying agency, such as a professional association or a national board.

You already may have invested in one or more degrees and may not want to invest in another. Or perhaps you are not interested in a college degree and prefer a vocational training option. No matter what your situation, you will enhance your resume by obtaining additional training and certifications in your preferred field. This chapter shares non-degree options that could make a positive difference in your federal job search.

"For many people a job is more than an income—it's an important part of who we are. So a career transition of any sort is one of the most unsettling experiences you can face in your life."

Paul Clitheroe, Australian media commentator on financial issues

The good news is quite a few reasonably priced and sometimes free certifications and training classes are available through a variety of sources. Certifications can be acquired in a relatively short timeframe, many in less than a year.

What Is Required Before Pursuing a Certification?

To qualify for many certifications, you need only a high school diploma. Don't have one? You can obtain a General Education Diploma (GED) at a low cost and sometimes for free through an adult education center. Contact your local community or junior college to locate the one nearest you. According to the American Council on Education (ACE), the organization that administers the test, "more than 95 percent of U.S. employers consider GED graduates the same as traditional high school graduates in regard to hiring, salary, and opportunity for advancement."

Test-takers must set aside time to prepare for the GED, which includes a challenging battery of tests. Preparation can take place in a classroom setting, through at-home study guides, or with TV and online resources. The test must be taken at an official ACE testing center (more than 3,000 available nationwide). Search for a GED testing center at www.acenet.edu/resources/GED/center_locator.cfm.

Sources for New Skills and Certifications

The Workforce Investment Act (WIA), passed in 1998, ensures that postsecondary educational institutions provide certifications and training classes under their adult education programs. One-Stop Career Centers are also funded by WIA, and they, too, offer certifications. As the term *one stop* suggests, One-Stop Career Centers provide a comprehensive collection of career services delivered in one place. The centers offer a limited number of certification options, but each certification is provided at no cost to the participant. Here is a link to One-Stop Career Centers across the country: www.careeronestop. org/JobSearch/COS_jobsites.aspx. This website and the One-Stop Career Centers are funded by the U.S. Department of Labor.

Another great place to search for skill development and certification options is at a nearby community or junior college (two-year campus). Some four-year colleges in rural areas offer such classes as well. Through WIA funding, state-funded colleges offer workforce development classes at a reasonable price. However, some of these colleges offer only GED-related education. The decision about the certification and training a college offers is based on the community's greatest need and the funding available to address it.

In addition to offering adult education certificates, two-year colleges often offer Certificates of Study and Letters of Recognition for credited majors. Course fees remain the same as other credit courses. However, each required course is an upper-division class. Basic education classes such as Speech, Psychology, and History are not required to receive these credentials. Some of these certificates require up to 30 college credits, so obtaining them will take some time.

The University of Texas (UT) at Austin offers an up-to-date and inclusive list of community and junior colleges by state: www.utexas.edu/world/comcol/state/. From here you can search for the two-year college nearest you.

 "You are never given a wish without the power to make it true. You may have to work for it, however."

Richard Bach, author

Four-year colleges often offer professional certifications to enhance your status within your chosen field. These certifications typically are not funded through WIA, and they can be expensive. For example, fees for credentials such as the Human Resource Management certification might range from $2,000 to $3,000 depending on your choice of advanced courses.

The University of Austin also offers a list of four-year U.S. colleges and universities by state, including private colleges and universities: www.utexas.edu/world/univ/state/.

Finally, colleges provide preparatory courses for GED, MCSE/MSCA, A+, and so on. However, students pay a separate fee to take the certifying exam. Some exams are quite expensive, so check to determine the certifying process offered by the college before you invest in a class. You want to avoid surprises such as finding out after the course has ended that you will need to make a further investment before you can attain the certification you are seeking.

For-profit colleges and for-profit technical/vocational schools do not receive WIA funding, so they do not offer the classes and certifications mentioned in this book.

Searching for Information on Certifications and Classes

After you identify your nearest two-year college, search its website using terms such as Workforce Development, Adult Education, or Community Education. Colleges may have slightly different names for this category, but all two-year colleges provide adult or community outreach education. Some adult education classes are for fun or for general knowledge, so don't be surprised if you run across a dog-training or basket-weaving class. Keep searching for classes that lead to a certificate or certification. Sometimes these classes are located under a title such as Center for Business and Training or a similar name.

Community college offerings might include such classes as A+ (IT), American Society for Quality (CMQ), Building Maintenance Engineer, Cisco Certified Networking Associate (CCNA), Electrical Training, HVAC/R (Heating, Ventilating, and Air Conditioning), Human Resource Management (SHRM Certification), International Public Management Association (IPMA), Law Enforcement (Police Academy), Payroll Professional (APA Certification), Pharmacy Technician, Phlebotomy Technician, Stationary Engineer/Boiler Operator, and/or Welding.

 "A strong economy begins with a strong, well-educated workforce."

Bill Owens, author

Information on how to obtain these certificates is located on the college website. Should you have difficulty finding this information, consider telephoning the college. Chances are they are eager to add students to their classes and will find a way to support your efforts.

Locating the certifications offered by four-year colleges could prove a challenge. Some four-year colleges do not offer certifications. Others offer them using terms such as Continuing Education, University Extension, Professional Development, or Community Education. For example, a nearby private university offers certifications through its Center for Continuing and Professional Education. You'll need to research the college nearest you to identify the terms they use and take it from there. Certifications may include executive coaching, leadership, organizational management, and performance management. Tenacity and a willingness to keep searching should finally yield the information you want. Otherwise, you can telephone the college.

Examples of Specific Colleges and Their Certifications

Following are eight geographically representative two- and four-year colleges with links to their certificate sites and lists of the adult education training/certifications they offer:

- **Borough of Manhattan Community College (BMCC)**
  http://bmcc.augusoft.net/index.cfm?fuseaction=1010

  Administrative Professional, Adobe Creative Suite, Bookkeeping with QuickBooks, Construction Programs, Entrepreneurship and Management, Film and Video Editing, Financial Planning, GED Preparation, Healthcare Programs, Information Technology, Microsoft Office, Paralegal Studies Program, Project Management, Supply Management

"No other investment yields as great a return as the investment in education. An educated workforce is the foundation of every community and the future of every economy."

Brad Henry, Oklahoma Governor

- **Georgetown University (GU)** http://scs.georgetown.edu/departments/5/center-for-continuing-and-professional-education/programs.cfm

  Budget and Finance, Business Administration, Business and Professional English, Corporate Executive Leadership, Digital Media Management, Diversity Strategy, Financial Planning, Forensic Accounting, Franchise Management, Government Executive Leadership, International Business Management, International Migration Studies, Leadership Coaching, Marketing, Nonprofit Management, Organizational Consulting and Change Leadership, Paralegal Studies, Project Management, Strategy and Performance Management

- **Kent State** www.kent.edu/yourtrainingpartner/index.cfm

  Accounting, ASQ, Autism Spectrum Intervention, Continuous Quality Improvement, Health Care, Human Resource Professional, ISO/QS/TS, Knowledge Management, Leadership, Lean Six Sigma, Library and Information Science, Nursing Education, Organizational Development, Project Management, Public Administration, Public Health, Small Business, Supervision/Management, Transition Specialist Endorsement

- **San Antonio College** www.alamo.edu/sac/ce/index.html

  Auditors Exam Preparation, Certified Corporate Trainer, Certified Nursing Assistant and Nursing Refresher, Child Development Associate, Computer Information Systems, Dental Assistant, Emergency Medical Services,

English as a Second Language Test Preparation, GED Preparation, Human Resource Management, Insurance Adjustor Preparation, Law Enforcement, Leadership and Management, Medical Administration and Technology Support, Monitor Technician, Project Management, Teacher Certificate

- **Seattle Central Community College** www. centralcertificates.com/Home_Page.html

  3-D Gaming, AutoCAD, Bookkeeper, Entrepreneurial Business Development, Grant Writing, National Personal Trainer, Nutritional Therapist, Paralegal, Sustainable Building Advisor, TESOL—Teach English to Speakers of Other Languages Program

- **University of California at Berkley** http://extension. berkeley.edu/

  Accounting, Alcohol and Drug Abuse Studies, Business Administration, Business Analysis, Clinical Research Conduct and Management, College Admissions and Career Planning, Construction Management, Entrepreneurship and Small Business Management, Essentials of Green Chemistry, Finance, Human Resource Management, HVAC, Integrated Circuit Design and Techniques, Interior Design and Interior Architecture, Landscape Architecture, Management, Marketing, Post-Baccalaureate Certificate in Information Systems and Management, Post-Baccalaureate Certificate in Visual Arts, Post-Baccalaureate Certificate Program in Writing, Project Management, Teaching English as a Second Language, UNIX/Linux System Administration

- **University of Minnesota Duluth** www.d.umn.edu/ce/ learningopportunities/certificates/index.html

  American Sign Language, Autism Spectrum Disorders, Educational Computing and Technology, Environmental

Education, Fetal Alcohol Spectrum Disorders, General Business Administration, Geographic Information Science, Human Services

- **Valencia Community College** www.valenciaenterprises. org/continuingeducation.cfm

Accounting and Tax; Business Communication; Consulting Financial Services; Customer Service; Emergency Management; Engineering; GED Testing/Test Preparation; Government; Human Resources; Language and Culture Leadership; Management; Manufacturing; Meeting Services; Office Administration; Public Safety Healthcare; Sales, Marketing, and Small Business; Supervision; Supply Chain Technology; Trades and Industrial

Online Adult Education Classes

Many colleges offer online adult education classes using a system called ed2go. Ed2go offers a library of approximately 300 training courses, some of which prepare students for testing in a variety of certifications, including the GED. These courses can be accessed from any computer, making it easy for most people to use the system no matter how remote their location or how busy their lifestyle. See the ed2go catalog at www. ed2go.com/CourseCatalog.aspx.

Closing Thoughts

Obtaining certifications and taking courses through adult education or professional development programs at local colleges offers a practical solution for acquiring additional skills to improve your resume for a federal job.

CHAPTER 9

CREATING YOUR CAREER PLAN

You have looked inward to discover who you are, what you like, and how work fits into your life. You learned about federal agencies so that you can find a match that enables you to reach your goals as well as contribute fully to the organizational mission. You have discovered the primary skills that the government is seeking and reviewed the qualifications of in-demand occupations with your federal job fit in mind. You have assessed your strengths and learned how to fill the education and skills gaps that stand between you and the realization of your potential.

> "All successful people have a goal. No one can get anywhere unless he knows where he wants to go and what he wants to be or do."
>
> *Norman Vincent Peale, minister and author*

Now it is time to put your unique talents, skills, and abilities into a career plan before you begin your search for the right federal job—a job where you can shine because it is your best federal fit.

Putting It All Together

At this point you can put all of the information you've learned together to project into your future. With an idea of the work you want to do, you will create a plan to reach the goal. Goal accomplishment becomes more possible when you have developed a plan for achieving it. Review your career goal information in chapter 4 and complete the following:

My career goal is to _____,
which uses my core values of _____,
_____, and _____
and utilizes the skills of _____,
_____, and _____ that I look
forward to doing every day. I will do this work in an agency
whose purpose and mission is to _____
_____.

Pursuing Your Dreams

A pitfall for many people is giving up before they have investigated the potential of their dreams. They are defeated before they have explored their options. Often they decide that they don't have what it takes to live their dreams. This is a short-sighted approach to potential possibilities. Rather than trust their intuition that they can utilize their strengths and interests to pursue meaningful work that pays the bills, they often allow negativism, their own as well as that of others, to derail their dreams. Somewhere it seems they have learned not to trust themselves.

 "Your vision will become clear only when you look into your heart. Who looks outside, dreams. Who looks inside, awakens."

Carl Jung, psychiatrist

Give yourself permission to dream, act on these dreams, and build them into your career plan. At this point, set your sights high and resist attempts, yours and others, to override your dreams.

Following are some techniques to develop and pursue your plan. This can be especially helpful if you experience barriers to accomplishing your goals. To keep moving in the direction of your choosing, you may wish to pursue some or all of the following methods for support and guidance.

Using SMART Goal Setting

The acronym SMART is a useful tool to help ensure that you are setting goals that are within your reach. SMART goals are specific, measurable, action-oriented, and realistic, and you have the time and resources to accomplish them.

Specific

What are you going to do? Your goal should be well-defined and clearly stated so that it is evident to anyone exactly what you wish to accomplish. Use action words to focus your path and to create clarity with your goal.

Example: "To become an information technology (IT) specialist, specializing in IT security."

Your turn. Goal: _____

_____

_____

Measurable

Describe exactly how you will know when you have accomplished the goal. Make the goal performance-based to ensure that the accomplishment of the goal is within your realm of possibility. People often make the mistake of establishing goals that are outcome-based, meaning that the result is dependent on others for its accomplishment, rather than within their own control.

For example, "establishing connections with five new networking contacts this week" is performance-based, because it is up to you and your own performance on whether this goal is achieved. "Finding a job by the end of the year" is outcome-based, because you have no control over whether it happens.

Example: "To submit a college application by March 31, 20XX."

Your turn. Measurable: _____

_____

_____

Action-Oriented

You must take initiative to move in the direction of your goal. The power of this step is that its completion propels forward movement. In other words, action begets action.

Example: "Research local colleges and identify two- and four-year colleges that offer a major or concentration in IT security."

Your turn. Action: _____

_____

_____

"If one advances confidently in the direction of one's dreams, and endeavors to live the life which one has imagined, one will meet with a success unexpected in common hours."

Henry David Thoreau, author

Realistic

Is your goal reasonable and possible to accomplish? Realistic goals keep you moving in the direction of your goal. When your goal is realistic, you are motivated to keep going because the goal is possible. If you become discouraged and find that you have lost enthusiasm for your goal, then you may have established a goal that is not achievable. Your goal is unrealistic when you have set your sights higher than your situation allows, which gives you an excuse to give up without trying.

Example: "Maintain a GPA that meets eligibility requirements for my college of choice."

Your turn. Realistic: _____

_____

_____

Time and Resources Available

In this step you determine whether you possess the wherewithal to accomplish your goal.

For example, if you are entering college to prepare for your first career, you typically have the available time to complete a degree. Conversely, if you are well established in your career, you need to decide whether you want to invest the amount of time and funds it will take to obtain additional certifications.

Example: "I have the time and funds available to obtain a degree/certification in IT security."

Your turn. Time and resources available: _____

_____

_____

Identifying Barriers to Reaching Your Goal

There may be barriers to achieving your goal, and to the extent possible you want to identify them and be aware of them so they do not derail your plans. For example, a barrier to becoming an IT security specialist may be that you are unable to gain admission to a four-year college and that you will need to start at a two-year college. In the space below, consider possible barriers to achieving your goal, and how you might overcome them.

Example. Barrier: "My poor grades in high school." How to overcome: "I will begin my college education at a two-year college and earn a high enough grade point average to allow me to transfer to a four-year college."

Your turn:

Barriers   How to Overcome

_____   _____

_____   _____

_____   _____

_____   _____

Using Affirmations to Achieve Your Goals

Often the barriers to achieving your goals are the negative messages you give yourself. In this case, you are your own enemy because you have defeated your attempts to be successful before anyone else knows your plans!

Using affirmations can be helpful. Affirmations are positive statements expressed in the present tense. They are written and verbalized as if they have already occurred. For example, "I am a successful teacher of fifth graders on U.S. military bases overseas" versus "I hope to become a fifth grade teacher for the military."

The power of affirmations is that they prepare your mind and your psyche for the possibilities that await you. Affirmations open the potential for the future by allowing you to see your goal actually occurring, rather than being so future oriented that your goal does not seem real. Affirmations also allow you to focus positively and keep you moving in the direction of your goal, rather than allowing you to be sabotaged by the negative messages you may hear from yourself and others.

Your turn. Affirmation: _____

_____

_____

 "Whether you think that you can, or that you can't, you are usually right."

Henry Ford, founder of Ford Motor Company

Using Visualization to Reach Your Goals

Set your sights high. Create an image of yourself as you want to be. Project this image into the future and actually "see" yourself in that role, engaged in the activities of the role. This technique is used by successful athletes, in which they see themselves in their mind's eye accomplishing their goal successfully. For example, the basketball player sees himself making that 3-point shot that wins the game, and the swimmer sees herself reaching the end of the pool before anyone else.

Your turn. See yourself accomplishing your career goal. Focus on the outcome. Visualize the endpoint.

"The future belongs to those who believe in the beauty of their dreams."

Eleanor Roosevelt, First Lady of the United States from 1933 to 1945

Staying Motivated

What keeps you moving in the direction of your goals? What fuels you? What drives you? What gets you out of bed in the morning? What do you want to accomplish? What keeps you going despite all odds? How do you characterize what gets you going?

For example, if your goal is to be a teacher, does your motivation originate from your childhood experiences? Perhaps your fifth-grade teacher was a model for you, and you saw yourself in that role, instructing and caring about the learning of young children. Perhaps your family was in the military when your teacher made a positive impression on you.

People can be motivated by extrinsic (external) rewards, such as salary, awards, or promotions. The possibility of these rewards enables them to continue to improve their performance or their outcomes.

Motivation can also be intrinsic; it comes from within. In this case, self-growth is self-determined, motivated by achievement and not by the expectations of others. Determining where your motivation comes from is an important factor in identifying how to set and achieve goals.

Spend a few moments considering where your motivation lies. Are you satisfied to pursue your goals whether you receive acknowledgment or recognition from others?

❑ Yes

❑ No

If yes, spend a few moments recalling a time when you pursued a goal without others' recognition:

_____

_____

_____

If no, explore an experience in which recognition from others motivated you to follow your goals:

_____

_____

_____

Stretching to Create Your Future

Step out of your comfort zone and the negative messages of others and possibly the negative messages you give yourself. Believe in yourself and let your dreams soar you above the crowds. You can be mediocre by constantly trying to remedy your weaknesses, or you can be exceptional by knowing your strengths and leveraging them.

 "All your dreams can come true if you have the courage to pursue them."

Walt Disney, film producer and co-founder of Walt Disney Company

If you are no stranger to self-doubt, you will question your ability to create and live your vision. It is the self-doubt that will prevent you from creating your future. Don't give in to it!

Writing Your Career Plan

At this point, you are able to commit your career plan to writing.

My goal is _____

Some barriers include _____

_____

_____

The type of agency I am seeking is _____

_____

I will accomplish this goal by the following date: _____

_____

My immediate steps include _____

_____

_____

_____

I will utilize the following resources (such as time, finances, assets, connections): _____

_____

_____

_____

Other factors I may need to consider (such as family issues, education, competing priorities):

_____

_____

Closing Thoughts

Your career plan is key for achieving the right federal job fit. In the next part, you will learn about federal job search strategies.

PART V

GETTING A
FEDERAL JOB

CHAPTER 10

THE FEDERAL JOB APPLICATION PROCESS— WORTH THE EFFORT

Many people believe that the federal job search process is so confusing and overwhelming that they decide not to make the effort. In assuming this attitude, they give up without trying. It is true that the system can be confusing, but with so many federal positions, generous benefits, and excellent job security, we suggest you view the process as an opportunity. This is especially important because many jobs will fit your interests, skills, and purpose for working.

This chapter demystifies the federal job application process.

Federal Hiring Reform

President Obama's memorandum dated May 11, 2010, "Improving the Federal Recruitment and Hiring Process," heralded sweeping change in how the federal government recruits and hires applicants. Responding to complaints that the process was unwieldy and cumbersome and didn't yield the highest quality selections, hiring reform purports to make the process easier and more transparent by eliminating KSAs (knowledge, skills, and abilities essays) as part of the application process, permit the resume and cover letter to be the primary vehicles when applying for a federal job, encourage more management accountability in the process, and require applicant notification of status several times during the process. These changes, which have been implemented with varying degrees of rigor across the government, suggest that you should pay special attention to the documents that you prepare in your submission package for a federal job.

Analyzing a Vacancy Announcement

The first step toward federal job search success is learning how to read a federal vacancy announcement (sometimes called a *job opportunity announcement* or *job opening announcement*) effectively. You will find quite a bit of jargon as you work your way through the announcement. However, with a little help you can begin to identify and decode standard information on each announcement you review.

Because a federal application requires a commitment of your time, make sure you meet the qualifications listed in the vacancy announcement before you spend the resources developing an application package.

Anatomy of a Vacancy Announcement

Federal vacancy announcements begin with an overview. The overview section includes relevant data for determining if you are interested in applying and whether you are eligible to apply. The overview is followed by a description of required duties, the experience and education needed to be considered most qualified, how your application package will be evaluated, federal benefits and other important information, and a very important section called How to Apply.

No matter where you scroll on the vacancy announcement page on USAJOBS.gov, a "questions about this job" section is located to the right. Feel free to contact the listed phone number any time you have concerns, especially if you need to have federal jargon interpreted. The number connects you to the human resources office, so you will not be interrupting the hiring official when you call.

A detailed description of the sections of an announcement follows.

Overview

The overview section provides a summary of the position and includes the salary range; the period during which applications are accepted; series and grade; whether the position is full-time, part-time, temporary, or permanent; location of the position; and who is eligible to apply. Pay special attention to the item called Who May Be Considered. It indicates the applicants who are eligible to apply. Do not confuse eligible with qualified. Read on until you reach the qualifications and evaluations section of the announcement for important information relevant to job seekers who are qualified for the job.

Duties

In the duties section, you will learn the tasks and primary responsibilities of the position. Pay special attention here. Include the terminology from the duties section in your resume and essays if you have any of the experience listed.

Qualifications and Evaluations

This very important portion of the announcement provides detailed information about the qualifications of the position and how applications are evaluated. Careful and thorough analysis of this section is vital for determining whether you are qualified for the job. It is crucial to include the terminology and keywords from this section in your application materials to specifically target your package to the position. Pay special attention to the area called Specialized Experience. If you do not possess this experience, you may wish to reconsider your decision to apply. This portion of the announcement specifically tells you what you need to possess to be considered qualified for the job. The evaluations part of this section includes information on criteria used to evaluate your application.

Benefits and Other Information

Here you receive information on the benefits available to you should you obtain the job, as well as additional information such as various locations for positions.

How to Apply

This section is your list of instructions on how to apply (for example, electronic submission only or hard copy acceptable). You will also be directed to submit certain documents as part of the application (for example, college transcripts or DD-214 [report of separation for veterans]). Pay careful attention to what is required, or your application may be rejected for incompleteness.

Writing a Cover Letter for a Federal Job

A cover letter for a federal job accompanies a hard copy resume. Providing a summary of credentials targeted to the job entices the recipient to read the resume for more information. Summarize the highlights of your resume and experience, rather than repeat what is contained in your resume. A cover letter is a marketing document that presents your experience in terms that are directly relevant to the job posting. It is your opportunity to sell your experiences and highlight your accomplishments on one page. Demonstrate that you have done some research about the agency. The cover letter does not have to be extensive, but it demonstrates that you have invested time to consider the position and put effort into writing this letter.

Economy of words and language that reflects your knowledge of the job is important in a cover letter. Spend the time to develop a document that portrays your unique qualifications for the job in a manner that is clear, concise, and cogent to get your resume the attention it deserves.

State that you would welcome a personal interview to discuss this opportunity. You might mention that if you do not hear anything in two to three weeks, you will call to follow up to see where the agency is in the hiring process. Finish by thanking the reader for his or her attention and expressing a desire meet to the person sometime in the near future.

Cover Letter Format

Your Street
City, State, Zip Code
Date

Employer's Name
Title
Name of Agency
Street
City, State, Zip Code

Dear Mr./Ms._____ (first and last names):

First Paragraph
In this first section of the cover letter, attract the reader's attention and kindle interest
to read further. Indicate the title of the position you are applying for, where you learned
about the position, and why you are interested in it.

Second Paragraph
In this paragraph, sell your qualifications, education, and experience and match them
to the requirements of the job. Explain the skills and experiences you have that will
make you successful in the position. Include classes you have taken and any volunteer
experience related to the position. Do not repeat what is contained in your resume.
Mention one or two of your qualifications for the position. Entice your reader to
continue reading by highlighting top accomplishments. Remember who your audience
is and target your information to that person's interests (that is, the reason he or she
would be interested in your qualifications). The goal is to show the employer that you
have confidence in your ability to succeed in the position.

Third Paragraph
This is the call to action of your letter. Begin by reiterating your interest in the job and
the agency, followed by your desired expectation of being contacted for an interview.
Provide all contact information so the reader can reach you. Include your e-mail
address, cell phone number, and home phone number.

Sincerely,

Signature

Typed Name

Enclosure: Resume

Sample Cover Letter

999 Key Highway
New York, NY 12345
March 23, 20XX

Mr. Albert Cross
Assistant Director
Division of Health Sciences
Bureau of Health Professions
2810 N. South Avenue
Baltimore, MD 44444

Dear Mr. Albert Cross:

I am interested in applying for the position of Patient Education Coordinator, which I learned about from the advertisement in my alumni newsletter, *The Clarion*. I have a great deal of experience in several aspects of patient education. It is a profession that I have come to love, and I have much to offer.

In my current position as Health Educator at Marymount Hospital, I am directly responsible for all aspects of patient education on the cardiac rehabilitation unit. This requires that I remain current in all areas of cardiac care, as well as nutrition, exercise, and other facets of health and wellness. My training programs have received national acclaim. I have developed materials to educate the nursing and medical staffs throughout the hospital. The success of my materials can be measured by a decreased length of hospital stay for patients who were admitted for cardiac problems. As part of my master's thesis, I created a program to educate teenagers about the dangers of texting and driving. Many of the points that I addressed in my thesis were adopted by several PTAs in the state. I have been told that my passion for empowering patients with information is contagious.

I would welcome the opportunity to meet with you in person. Please feel free to contact me at sjones@gmail.com, at 222-222-2222 (cell phone), or at 111-111-1111 (home phone). Thank you for considering my application, and I look forward to speaking with you soon.

Sincerely,

Sally Jones

Sally Jones

Enclosure: Resume

Writing a Federal Resume

A federal resume is a detailed summary of your education and experience, tailored to the job for which you are applying. Do not make the common mistake of sending a generic two-page resume to apply for a federal job. These resumes do not include the information federal human resource analysts need to maintain required records. Such resumes cannot earn enough rating points to be competitive. Federal human resource analysts carefully review the federal resume to award rating points based on preset criteria. The application packages earning the highest number of rating points are sent to the hiring manager for consideration.

A federal resume can be up to six pages long, and it contains certain required information:

- Information obtained from the vacancy announcement

    Announcement number

    Position title

    Job grade

- Your personal information

    Full name

    Mailing address

    Day and evening telephone numbers

    E-mail address

    Social Security number

    Country of citizenship

Veterans' preference (if applicable)

Reinstatement eligibility

Highest federal civilian grade held

- Past and current work experience

  Job title

  Starting and ending dates (include months)

  Employer's name, city, state

  Average number of hours worked

  Supervisor's name and phone number or e-mail address. You must also indicate whether the supervisor can be contacted.

  Describe experience that is relevant to the job you are applying for to create a tailored resume. As indicated earlier, include terminology and keywords from the duties and qualifications portions of the announcement, if relevant to your background. Do not include information that is older than 10 years, unless it is directly relevant to the job. Any type of experience that is relevant to the job should be included (for example, paid, unpaid, internships, federal, and non-federal).

  In a federal resume, it is important to describe not only what tasks you performed but also the outcomes of your contributions. In other words, provide detailed information regarding how your efforts impacted the job and the organization. Be as specific as possible, and where possible, quantify your accomplishments (for example, money saved and process streamlined).

- Education

    Without college. If you have no college experience, list the name, city, and state of your high school and the date you received a diploma or GED. It is not necessary to include information about high school if you have completed college coursework unless the hiring agency requests it.

    With college. List the name, city, and state of the college or university. List major(s), type, and year of degree(s). Include specific coursework related to the job. Include your GPA if it is at least 3.0 on a 4.0 scale.

To obtain additional rating points on a federal resume, include information about awards, professional affiliations, and training.

Sample Federal Resume

JOHN ADAMS
367 Albermarle Place, Georgetown, LA 12345
435-555-1212 (H) ▪ 435-667-9999 (C) ▪ jadams@hmail.com

Social Security Number: 123-45-6789	Country of Citizenship: United States
Highest Grade: N/A	Veterans' Preference: None

Position Applied For: Staff Accountant, GS-510-11/12/13
Announcement Number: 10-2263-HQ-MD-D1

PROFESSIONAL PROFILE

Quality-driven professional with strong organizational skills. Analytical thinker. Able to make effective decisions in a fast-paced environment. Highly motivated to achieve excellence with ability to motivate others. Exceptional interpersonal skills. Enthusiastic and versatile presenter.

AREAS OF STRENGTH

Detail oriented, problem solver, ability to manage several tasks simultaneously.

SPECIAL SKILLS

Proficiency with Microsoft Office Suite, Internet research, excellent communication skills, Intuit QuickBooks software.

EMPLOYMENT HISTORY

Financial Management Analyst, no grade level   5/2008–present
STG, Inc., Washington, DC 21000
Hours per week: 40
Supervisor: Barbara Jones, 202-555-1212 (may be contacted)
Provide support and guidance to a federal contractor in the implementation of an accounting system for the federal government. Possess knowledge of federal accounting principles. Serve as a key player in the development of processes that created a smooth transition between systems.
- Assist in preparing weekly and monthly financial reports, including summaries of policy review, to provide expert guidance and analysis.
- Develop relationships with colleagues to expedite the flow of information.
- Streamline the process of providing updates to management by creating internal monitoring systems using Excel spreadsheets.
- Effectively communicate orally and in writing and prepare and deliver monthly reports and briefings to higher management for use in decision making.
- Coordinate the implementation of financial management policies.

Customer Support Specialist, no grade level   9/2002–5/2008
Federal Management Systems, Inc., Washington, DC 21000
Hours per week: 40
Supervisor: Mike Smith, 202-555-1111 (may be contacted)
Provided administrative support regarding the program objectives and management of telecommunication technologies. Exercised judgment and reason and relieved supervisor of as many administrative duties as possible. Recognized as a go-to person for resolving customer complaints with tact and diplomacy.
- Prepared final correspondence with recommendations for management signature and approval.
- Resolved customer complaints using own judgment and fact finding.
- Utilized knowledge of basic financial procedures and processes to track a wide variety of program expenses.
- Checked to ensure that appropriate changes were made to resolve customers' problems.

(continued)

(continued)

JOHN ADAMS, 123-45-6789, 10-2263-HQ-MD-D1   Page 2

EDUCATION

University of Maryland, College Park, MD
Robert Smith School of Business
Bachelor of Arts in Accounting, received May 2008
Recipient of National Society of Public Accountants (NSPA) Scholarship
Maintained a 3.4/4.0 GPA while working throughout college

Relevant Courses
Principles of Accounting I (3 credits), Intermediate Accounting I (3 credits), Managerial Accounting (3 credits), Taxation of Individuals (3 credits)

TRAINING AND CERTIFICATION

- Certificate of Completion, Introduction to Federal Accounting, The Graduate School, 2008
- Leadership and Management Certification, Academy of Leadership, University of Maryland, 2010-2011, 120 hours

SPECIAL AWARD

Top Achiever, Robert Smith School of Business, University of Maryland, 2008

PROFESSIONAL AFFILIATION

Member, National Society of Public Accountants, 2008 – present

---

Writing Personal Essays

Although one of hiring reform's tenets is the elimination of application essays, they are still very much in evidence on many vacancy announcements. This is primarily because the OPM, as the federal government's human resources office, does not have the power to mandate compliance with recommendations. The authority for making the recommended changes is delegated to each agency, resulting in uneven adoption of the principles of hiring reform across government.

Therefore, you can expect to see personal essays as a requirement in many job postings. They may be called KSAs, competency statements, application essays, or quality rating factors. They are all terms for personal essays, which address your particular knowledge, skills, and abilities as they relate to the position for which you are applying:

- Knowledge. An organized body of information, usually of a factual or procedural nature, that when applied, makes adequate job performance possible.

- Skill. The proficient manual, verbal, or mental utilization of data, people, or things. Skills are observable, quantifiable, and measurable.

- Ability. The power to perform a given activity.

An application essay is usually a one-page document that highlights your accomplishments relevant to the job for which you are applying. It is your opportunity to showcase your achievements and can make the difference between an application package that results in being invited for an interview — or not. Spend sufficient time on these essays so that you demonstrate the highlights of your career and show that you are the most qualified applicant for the job.

As first introduced in chapter 1, here is the CCAR formula you may wish to follow when writing your essays:

- Context. Describe the specific problem you had to address. What did you solve, resolve, respond to, and handle?

- Challenge. Describe the factors that contributed to a particular challenge, such as budget cuts, new legislation, institutional reform, and new goals from upper management.

- Action. Describe the steps you took to solve the problem. Stay away from the ordinary—be extraordinary in your response!

- Result. Describe the outcome of your actions in quantifiable terms. Use percentages, numbers, grades, amounts. Emphasize the difference you made.

In this manner, you demonstrate clearly to the reader what value you brought to your job by the unique manner in which you confronted the problem, the actions you employed to overcome the situation, and the demonstrable results you achieved. You are showing, through real-life examples, your unique contribution. Your uniqueness and its illustration are vital, so long as you convey them in a manner that is relevant to the position for which you are applying.

If you spend sufficient time to create clearly worded essays that convey your contributions, you have begun preparing for the interview, which is your opportunity to showcase your accomplishments in person.

Sample KSAs

Each agency determines which KSAs it wants addressed in the federal application package. The following KSAs are examples of possible essays for a supervisory contract specialist (1102 series), supervisory procurement analyst (1101 series), or budget analyst (0560 series).

Knowledge and skill in customer service and client relations.

Throughout my career, I have been commended by peers, superiors, and senior-level managers for my expert ability to provide customer service and client relations. I utilize principles of the FISH philosophy: being present, being enthusiastic, and having a positive attitude and Civility, Respect, and Engagement in the Workplace (CREW) in both internal and external customer service. Difficult problems involve many key stakeholders, with interests particular to their given area of concern. These are often highly charged, emotional issues. I have a strong ability to both listen and hear messages conveyed by those I encounter in my work. Diffusing anger, anxiety, and stressful situations is a large part of my daily work. As a clinical nurse and manager of health services, I have dealt with sensitive issues involving legal issues, mental health issues, and matters of social concern. Maintaining a professional demeanor at all times is a hallmark of my practice, as is providing respect to my clients and their families. Providing accurate information and maintaining a spirit of partnership is essential in providing excellent customer service. I hold myself to a high level of responsibility and accountability to my superiors, co-workers, peers, and clients. I frequently bridge the distance between analytical and creative elements and persons. My expertise includes solving difficult problems, such as working with clients in worker's compensation case management, with substance abuse issues, with mental health lapses, and with chronic disease issues. Included in resolution of these matters is the observation of applicable acts, policies, and laws governing operation of the institution and community. Averting the advancement of difficult problems up the chain of command and addressing them at my level is often accomplished. Seeking service recovery when there is dissatisfaction with a clinic experience and seeking win-win solutions are tasks I perform on a frequent basis.

My expertise in customer service and client relations led to my involvement in and chairmanship of committees and task forces, such as the Safety Committee at Marydale Community College and the American College Health Association's Task Force on Affiliate Operations, which performed a three-year review of incorporation. Respect for individuality while collaborating on a plan and process was essential in meeting the goals of the task force.

As a master of public health intern, I supplied written detailed guidelines for procurement for the regional agency by developing quote estimates and proposed expenditures. Equal amounts of information needed to be shared within appropriate timelines. With multiple organizations competing for several grant processes, confusion was occurring. I took the initiative to meet personally with the procurement director to draft guidelines, submit them to my supervisors for approval, and then distribute them to each agency. This resulted in increased knowledge of the grant process and timeline and required supporting documentation. Improvements were noted in the reporting and reimbursement process following dissemination of this information.

Interpreting guidelines for groups, including ESF-8 specific interactions between local public health emergency preparedness officials, hospital preparedness officials, and emergency operations centers was a large component of my internship. I followed federal grant processes and assisted the East-West Gateway Council of Governments, state Department of Health and Senior Services, and local public health agencies in meeting purchasing and reimbursement guidelines for successful procurement and reimbursement of emergency public health preparedness resources. This involved a significant amount of customer service skill. Providing accurate, timely information and sharing equal amounts of information were key to good customer service and handling complicated matters. Utilizing management by objectives and closing the loop from funding processes to outcomes assessment were important to providing good service to all parties at all levels of government.

Ability to develop project budgets and monitor program expenditures.

At St. Albans Community College, I performed health service administration, budget, policy and procedure development, and strategic planning for a department serving 12,000 students, 300 employees, and 3 outreach education centers with a growth rate of 260 percent over a nine-year span.

The budgeting process included the following steps:

I developed, budgeted, and managed health programs, special projects, and events utilizing both operating budget and fee-for-service funds. My expertise in this area led to Maryview University recruiting me to rebuild the budgeting processes for the college health service, where my outstanding efforts resulted in a 7 percent merit pay raise after five months.

Working within a public institution, I worked with purchasing agents to create contracts, review requests for bids and vendor ratings, recommend contract awardees using public sector ratings, and purchase within budget guidelines.

Included in the project budget development process was my ability to plan a timeline with milestones and to meet deadlines for purchasing processes, including bid process and review prior to actual purchase of services. Researching costs, along with a percentage built in to stay under budget, was essential to my practice. My experience in budget management includes development and administration of service contracts, durable capital goods, and consumable supplies.

Frequent review and process evaluation with monthly reconciliation during the fiscal year was essential. I have never run over budget as a manager, and in fact during a state funding hold-back managed to provide continued quality of service while adjusting spending to keep departmental funding within budget and without cost overrun. As a project manager, I manage time, plot progressive goals, and estimate costs effectively.

Federal Networking Strategies

The federal government's hiring process and procedures are regulated by the Merit Systems Protection Board, resulting in many rules and regulations to maintain fairness and accessibility for all applicants. However, as in any job search campaign, it is always useful to employ networking techniques to find out about opportunities that you may not otherwise be aware of.

With hiring reform, managers and supervisors are encouraged to become more involved in the process. What this means for you as a job seeker is that you want to try to meet as many hiring officials (managers and supervisors) as possible who could help you get a job. You have many opportunities to get out and meet people and develop relationships with those who have the authority to hire in their agencies. Join a professional association in your industry, maintain a connection with your alumni association, and let people know that you are looking for a federal job. Networking and letting people know your interests are much easier when you have targeted an occupation or a federal agency. Target your elevator speech (from chapter 4) to the specific occupation you are seeking, and you're ready to go!

With networking, the expression "It's not what you know, it's who you know" becomes "It's not what you know, it's not who you know, it's who knows you." Make your contacts work for you, and make sure that you reciprocate. Do not become a symbol of what has been termed drive-by networking, in which the emphasis is on quantity of contacts rather than the quality of relationships. A crucial component of networking is building and nurturing relationships.

The theory of six degrees of separation puts forward the reality of connection between and among people. It states that only six contacts stand between you and anyone else. Therefore, if you approach your contacts and each of them connects with their contacts, by the sixth level, you would reach everybody.

To keep you energized and motivated for networking events, you might want to refresh your passion for work and your life purpose from chapter 4. Make sure that you convey that you are the right person for the job that you're targeting. Remember, if you are passionate about your reasons for seeking federal employment, you will make a favorable impression on a hiring manager, who is most likely a long-term public servant passionate about public service.

Creative Networking

The federal system sometimes seems closed, like it has a do-not-enter sign posted for people trying to network their way to jobs. However, savvy federal job seekers often find creative ways around the system. One idea is to work for a private-sector organization that contracts with federal agencies. Make sure during your interview that your worksite is co-located with your federal counterparts. You might want to ask for a tour of the workspace. Excellent contract workers often become go-to people and get noticed by federal hiring officials. A well-kept secret is that some contractors are asked to apply for federal jobs and subsequently are selected for a federal position. Such people still have to go through the federal hiring hoops and regulations, but extra care is taken to ensure that person's name gets included on the certificate of eligibles.

Another idea is to search agency websites for an employee directory. For example, for the Department of Health and Human Services, go to www.dhhs.gov and find its HHS Index A–Z. You will find an employee directory listed under E. For this particular directory, you need the last name or initial of the person you are seeking. The first 100 people (in the alphabet) who meet your search criteria will be shown on the list.

Completing a last-name-only search for the common name Johnson identified people with first names beginning with A through C. If you want to locate people farther down the alphabet, just complete a search using an initial for their first names. You can also complete a search using only the first initial of a last name. These searches identify only the first 100 people meeting your criteria, but that's 100 more than you had before. You might have to find creative ways to use this database, but contacting someone identified through this search could be a wonderful way to obtain an informational interview and begin to build your network of people working for the agency you are targeting.

Additional ways of searching this site include related organizations, job title, keywords, building (a list is provided), and city. A completed search identifies the employee's organization in HHS, job title, and duty station. Clicking on the link to the name provides a direct telephone number and e-mail address, two great ways of contacting a federal employee to request an informational interview.

You need to use such terms as *employee locator* or *employee directory* to search for the directory on an agency site. Not all agencies offer a directory. Other agencies may not provide a directory for the entire organization but offer directories for some sub-agencies. Search the website of the agency you are targeting to determine what is available. If you cannot locate an online employee directory, call the main number on the Contact Us page and ask if one exists. Be sure to get the site address if it does.

Another way to network your way to an informational interview with a federal employee is to review organizational charts. Most agencies have an easy-to-locate organizational chart on their About Us web page. Typically names are included on those charts and sometimes contact information as well. However, if no contact information is available, you can call the agency and ask to be connected to an individual. Keep in mind that the names on organizational charts are of high-level employees, so it might take some time to connect with them. Your chances of contacting them may be increased if you try early in the morning before they have been overtaken by the events of the day or late in the afternoon when most of the office staff has left for the day.

Social Networking

You can use social networking tools such as LinkedIn at www.linkedin.com. LinkedIn is currently the number one social networking site for professional and business purposes. Make sure you focus on what you really want so that your online network can boost your efforts!

Using LinkedIn to identify and connect with federal employees is a possibility. To do so, you must have your own LinkedIn account. You can complete a company search using "U.S.," and a number of federal agencies appear. Or search for the specific agency, such as FEMA, and its LinkedIn site will appear. Once there, view your LinkedIn connections to people already working there, see new hires with LinkedIn accounts, and identify all the agency employees who have LinkedIn accounts. From there you can get introduced to an agency employee, and you can begin networking for an informational interview. You might be surprised to learn how closely you are connected to someone who knows someone working for your targeted agency.

Federal Job Search Support Groups Online

Groups on LinkedIn can support your federal job search. One such group is the Federal Job Search Support group administered by Karol Taylor, an author of this book. Two other groups are the Federal Job Search Help group and the Federal Job Search Training Club. Investigate each group to determine which one best meets your needs. Some members of these groups have obtained federal jobs and want to help others in their federal job search.

LinkedIn has a feature that offers groups you might be interested in based on the groups you have already joined, so you might want to check them out, too. The idea is to get as much online support as possible and to begin networking your way to federal job search success.

Advantages of Social Networking

Social networking sites such as LinkedIn can exponentially increase your contacts electronically. Utilize this resource while maintaining your personal connections with your network. Some advantages of social networking include

- Expanding your network of contacts.
- Finding jobs posted on LinkedIn.
- Researching organizations.
- Joining groups of people with similar interests.
- Posting questions and getting answers.
- Answering other people's questions, which can establish your online presence as an expert in your field.
- Searching for people in particular jobs or agencies.
- Posting a profile that others—such as connections or potential employers—can view.
- Strengthening professional relationships.

Managing Your Reputation

Your reputation is essentially the opinion and belief that others have about you. In chapter 4, we discuss the importance of creating your personal brand. A personal brand is a reflection of who you are and broadcasts what you stand for. It is a combination of your reputation and the emotions evoked toward you by others. In determining what image you wish to convey, know that your activities and actions must reinforce this image for your reputation to be consistent with your brand.

Pay special attention to your online presence. Make sure your social networking buttresses the image you want to convey and the self that you are promoting in your other marketing materials (such as your resume, cover letter, and application essay).

If this branding is difficult for you, and you are not sure what you want your brand to reflect about you, it may be helpful to go back to chapters 3 and 4 and review the self-exploration exercises. Your reputation is contingent on identifying and maintaining your image, which may require some more soul-searching and self-exploration. Everything that you say, do, and write promotes and reinforces your image. You can manage your reputation when you know what you want it to entail. Don't leave it to chance. Identify, cultivate, and nurture it beginning with an understanding of who you truly are.

Joining Professional Associations

One of the best ways to promote a professional identity and maintain your professional relevance is through membership in a professional association. In addition, professional associations provide opportunities for members to network. Membership conveys privileges such as attendance at conferences, professional development, and participation in local chapters. You may wish to volunteer to serve as an officer or in some other position that provides you with visibility as well as gives you an opportunity to develop your skills.

Membership in a professional association clearly states your professional identity, as well as demonstrating that you are interested in growing in your profession. It brands you as an expert in your field. Include your participation on your resume as another way to set yourself apart from the competition. Even better, enhance your brand by being an officer!

Distinguishing Yourself

As in all competitive situations, the key for federal job search success is to distinguish yourself. In chapters 3 and 4, you explored your skills, interests, passions, and motivations. You developed your mission statement, wrote your elevator speech, clarified your values, and identified your motivated skills. You pondered your personality, discovered your life purpose, and created your career goal.

This self-exploration, with the answers to the difficult questions you posed to yourself, can elevate you above the competition. By maintaining a professional identity that reflects who you are at your core can result in your achievement of professional success and satisfaction throughout your career.

Closing Thoughts

Applying for a federal job can be disheartening. But as stated at the beginning of the chapter, so many jobs will fit your interests, skills, and purpose that the pursuit of a federal job can be very worthwhile.

CHAPTER 11

INTERVIEWING FOR A FEDERAL JOB

Your application has warranted the next step in the federal job search process: an interview. Congratulations! A major aspect of any job search is the interview. Many people approach the interview with dread and trepidation and can sabotage their success through fear. However, with preparation, you can view the interview as your chance to have a mutually beneficial conversation with an employer who is looking for a good fit for a job opening. You, as the candidate, are also looking for a good fit for your skills, talents, interests, and passions.

By reframing your view of the interview from an interrogation to a conversation, you will be better able to regard your role as equal participant with as much to share and offer as the interviewer. In fact, career experts indicate that the interviewee can expect to provide at least 50 percent of the information in an interview, making it truly a give and take of receiving and exchanging valuable information.

Remember that you want a good fit as much as the employer wants the best hire. In this regard, you have as much at stake as the interviewer. Therefore, you are interviewing the interviewer as much as he or she is interviewing you. Make the most of the opportunity to find out enough about the organization and the job so that you can make a decision that is in your best interest.

Types of Interviews

You may participate in one or several types of interviews. When you are called about the interview, you may ask who will be interviewing you and what type of interview you can expect. Here is a listing of the most common types of interviews.

Phone

A phone interview is usually a screening, preliminary interview. It is often conducted to decide whether an applicant will be invited to an in-person interview. However, because of time and budget constraints, some agencies employ phone interviews for selection.

Panel

A panel interview involves more than one interviewer. Do not be intimidated; connect with each interviewer by making eye contact and establishing rapport. Some candidates report that they prefer this type of interview. They state that it is likely they can find a connection with at least one person, whereas in the individual interview you need to make a personal connection with only one person.

Traditional

In this type of interview, you may be asked some questions that require hypothetical responses. Examples of situational questions appear later in the chapter.

Stress

Although uncommon, this type of interview is so-called because it intentionally induces a stress-filled scenario to gauge how job seekers react. Some techniques for a stress interview include keeping the applicant waiting for an extended period of time, answering phone calls and responding to e-mails during the interview, or requiring the applicant to complete timed or problem-solving tasks. A stress interview would typically be used in a work environment that is fast-paced and multifaceted, and the employer needs to ensure that the selected applicant is able to perform in this atmosphere.

Competency-Based Structured/ Behavioral Approach

This type of interview assumes that the best predictor of future behavior is past performance under similar conditions. The behavior-based questions are posed in the context of competencies required to perform successfully in the job. See sample competency-based questions and behavioral questions later in this chapter. A structured interview requires that each candidate is asked the same questions, with responses rated and ranked after the interview. A detailed discussion of a structured interview appears next.

A variety of other methods may be used to evaluate candidates, including the following:

- A simulation places job seekers in situations that replicate the work environment.

- In a work samples evaluation, the candidate is given a specific task to accomplish during the interview.

- Through an assessment center, a variety of testing techniques allow candidates to demonstrate, under standardized conditions, the skills and abilities most essential for success.

- In their efforts to deemphasize the importance of application essays, some federal agencies initially review resumes only. If a resume lists the skills an agency is seeking, it then invites a candidate to write essays (KSAs). The quality of the essays determines whether the applicant will be invited to an interview. In this instance, following proper federal resume guidelines is essential.

Structured Interviews

Although federal departments and agencies are able to determine their own processes, many are employing structured interviews. In a structured interview, all candidates are asked the same questions in the same order to make the process fair for all. The questions are based on an analysis of the job. The interview questions are behavioral and situational and are set up to provide concrete, specific examples that indicate skills that you have used in the past.

Candidates are evaluated using a common rating scale, and interviewers agree on acceptable answers. A panel of usually three to five interviewers takes detailed notes and numerically evaluates responses. The panel can be made up of persons who have extensive knowledge of the job and are trained in administering interviews.

You can bring supplemental documents to the interview (for example, resume, transcripts, and references). This information is for your reference only and will not be looked at by the interviewers during the interview.

Interviewers will

- Welcome you in a warm and friendly manner.

- Thank you for your interest in the position and for coming to the interview.

- Briefly describe the job and relevant organizational characteristics to allow you to become comfortable.

- Explain the interview process in a standardized way.

- Inform you that notes will be taken throughout the interview.

- Ask if you have any questions before beginning.

Here's what to expect in the interview setting:

- Interviewers may provide the questions in writing to you.

- Interviews will be held in a quiet, nonthreatening, and private place.

- Seating arrangements are the same for all candidates.

- The interview room and facilities will be accessible to candidates with disabilities.

- There will be a separate area for those waiting to be interviewed.

- Individuals who have been interviewed will not be allowed to communicate with those waiting to be interviewed.

- All candidates will be allotted the same amount of interview time.

During the interview, interviewers will follow specific guidelines. The interviewer's guide provides general instructions about the interview process, a summary of common rating biases and rating mistakes to avoid, and general tips for good interviewing. The guidelines provide information specific to the particular interview, including

- Definitions of each competency being assessed
- Proficiency levels of each competency
- Interview questions
- Rating scales (with behavioral examples and/or representative responses) for each question
- Examples of probing questions

A probe is a question asked by the interviewer to help clarify a candidate's response or ensure the candidate has provided enough information. When necessary, the interviewer should ask similar probes for all candidates to ensure they are provided the same opportunities to respond. While probes may need to be tailored to address each candidate's specific response, the general meaning of the probes should not change.

At the end, the interviewer will

- Ask if you would like the interviewers to know anything else.
- Provide you an opportunity to ask questions.
- Thank and excuse you (make sure to wait for this to happen).

When you leave, the following will occur:

- The interviewers immediately will review their notes and rate your answers.

- Examples of actual answers given will be included in the interviewers' notes along with explanations of how these answers apply to the competency being rated and why they merit the rating given.

- The interviewers will discuss their ratings and come to a consensus.

Benefits of the structured interview are as follows:

- It is legitimate and reliable.

- It controls the flow of the interview.

- It addresses the candidates' concerns about being treated inequitably.

- It makes the interview the same for every candidate, which ensures equal opportunity.

- Similar competencies are evaluated in each interview, which controls reliability.

- Questions are pre-written, reducing nervousness for the interviewers.

- It maximizes the interviewers' time.

Stages of an Interview

Every interview is best viewed in three stages: before, during, and after. We discuss each stage separately, explaining the qualities and factors important in each.

Before the Interview

It is reported that many people who are well-qualified for positions enter interview situations ill-prepared to speak about their skills, interests, goals, and what contributions they might make to the job and agency. A helpful way to envision your role in the interview and the expectations of you as an interviewee is to consider that the interviewer is seeking a well-qualified individual to solve a problem or series of problems. Jobs exist because problems need to be solved. Think of yourself as a problem solver, bringing all of the resources and talents you possess to bear on the problem needing resolution.

Similarly, the interviewer, who is likely the hiring official, is seeking someone who can solve problems without too much preparation or on-the-job training. Therefore, to match your skills and talents with the employer's needs and wants, you must demonstrate your capabilities in such a manner that the employer can "see" you performing the job. Rather than being intimidated by the challenge of the interview process, instead view it as your opportunity to show yourself as the best person for the job. After all, you made it to the interview stage, having completed a rigorous application process! The interview is now your chance to articulate and demonstrate in person what you have successfully conveyed in writing.

The following provides some guidelines for interview preparation.

Review the Vacancy Announcement

Become familiar with the position. Understand its duties and qualifications and be able to articulate how you are uniquely qualified to fulfill the expectations of the job. Be able to discuss your qualifications in light of what you have included in your resume, providing additional information and details about your unique credentials for the job.

Research the Employer

Study the agency's website. Become familiar with the agency, its mission, and the department within which the agency is located. Find out the strategic plan of the organization and any trends or challenges that the organization is facing.

Review Your Resume and Any Questions You May Have Answered as Part of the Application

Review the application materials that you submitted for the position. The process you used to develop these materials is excellent practice for the interview. Be prepared to respond to questions about the content of your application. Also be prepared to provide greater detail with more success stories from your experience.

Identify Your Strengths and Weaknesses

When discussing your strengths, be prepared to present examples of when you demonstrated them. Have at least three strengths to discuss. Do not fall into the trap of being uncomfortable with "bragging" when you speak about what you have to offer. The interview is your chance to sell yourself and to prove that you are the best candidate for the job. A description of your strengths, spoken eloquently and confidently, will give the interviewer an impression of your comfort level with your abilities.

When you discuss weaknesses, provide strategies for overcoming them. This is your opportunity to demonstrate your awareness of areas for development. Avoid mentioning weaknesses that negatively impact your performance in the position. For example, discomfort with public speaking is a weakness that would not necessarily impact a web developer, but it would be a barrier to successful performance for an instructor. Be prepared to explain two weaknesses with strategies for improvement.

Example: *I am uncomfortable with public speaking, but I have joined Toastmasters International to develop my speech-giving ability.*

Highlight and Identify Accomplishments from Your Career and Personal Life

Accomplishments or success stories provide specific examples of what you did and the impact your efforts had on your previous employer.

Example: *I decreased customer complaints by 75 percent monthly by initiating the design of a new user-friendly installation package. I recommended and implemented a new customer hotline and software application, resulting in increased customer satisfaction and more timely resolution of customer complaints.*

Develop stories with examples to convey your accomplishments in CCAR (remember: Context, Challenge, Action, Result) format.

Anticipate Possible Interview Questions, Based on the Content of the Announcement

Depending on the agency, you may be asked questions related to criminal history, drug usage, and other security-related concerns either in the interview or at other times during the process. Be prepared to answer these questions truthfully and to undergo a background investigation and the associated adjudication process if offered a sensitive position.

Give Examples that Prove Your Skills and Competencies for the Job

This is the place to share a powerful story that presents your competencies in the best possible way. Follow these steps:

1. Identify competencies and skills from the keywords on the vacancy announcement.

2. Be prepared to provide examples of how you utilized those competencies and skills.

3. Develop your story. A good story

   - Starts with a problem, conflict, or challenge.

   - Describes a unique experience.

   - Describes your concrete actions.

   - Is short and simple.

   - Makes a point.

In your competency story, include examples of the top skills required for the position.

Develop and Practice Your Elevator Speech

In chapter 4, you developed your elevator speech, which is your personal branding statement that informs the listener of your unique qualities and how your qualities can enhance the interviewer and the organization. Creating this statement is important to help you define who you are, what you can do, and how you add value. The *process* of developing it is as important as the outcome and the content because you will go through a period of self-discovery as you create your two-minute personal pitch.

As in any other marketing materials you have prepared for your job search, the elevator speech should be tailored and targeted to each job. When the interviewer states, "Tell me about yourself" at the beginning of the interview, you will be ready with a prepared and polished pitch, practiced to the point that it sounds natural and unrehearsed.

Prepare Answers to the Most Common Interview Questions

Your responses to common questions will present your skills, talents, and accomplishments. Spend quality time preparing your responses to these questions:

- Why should I/we hire you?

- Tell me about yourself.

- Why did you leave your last position, or why are you leaving your current position?

- What do you know about our organization?

- What are your goals?

- Where do you see yourself in five years?

- Why would you like to work here?

- What is your most significant career achievement?

- How would your previous bosses and colleagues describe you?

Prepare at Least Three to Five Questions to Ask the Interviewer(s)

It is important to have questions for the interviewer(s). When you are asked, usually at the end of the interview, "Do you have any questions for me?," a response of "No, you have answered all my questions" is considered a sign of disinterest in the position. Well-thought-out and developed questions indicate that you are interested in the position and that you have invested the time to prepare questions to help you learn more about the job and the organization.

Following are some questions you may wish to ask, but you can certainly develop others:

- What are the responsibilities of this job? You may wish to ask for a position description, which specifically addresses the job's tasks.

- What percentage of time is spent on each task?

- How did this position become available?

- How is performance evaluated?

- What do you find compelling about working here?

- What are the goals of the office?

- How does this position help the organization meet its goals?

- Do you anticipate the position will change in the future? How?

Practice Your Interview!

Conduct a mock interview with a friend or family member and ask him or her to provide feedback on your responses. You don't want the first time that you say the words to be at the interview. If you are unable to find someone to assist you, practice in front of your mirror, out loud, so you know how you sound and what areas may need special attention and further preparation before the interview.

During the Interview

The second stage is when you are being interviewed. Here are key actions to minimize nervousness and anxiety:

- Be on time. Make sure you know where the interview will be held. Some job seekers find it helpful to conduct a dry run to be sure they can find the location.

- Shake hands, smile, be yourself. This will help you relax. Do not pretend to be someone or something you are not.

- Be pleasant to everyone you meet. Receptionists and secretaries may be asked for their opinion about you. Make sure that you create a favorable impression.

- Demonstrate a sincere interest in the organization and the position. If you are interested in the position, say so. Make it clear that you want the job.

- Be confident. This is not the time to feel squeamish about "bragging." You have been invited to the interview because you demonstrated your qualifications in writing.

- Use examples and stories from your background to heighten the interviewers' interest, to create a picture in his or her mind, and to be memorable.

- Focus on what you can contribute to the organization rather than on what the organization can do for you.

- Never make negative references to previous employers. Doing so will reflect negatively on you. If you have had problems with a supervisor, you can indicate that the job was not a good fit, rather than divulge specifics.

- Be aware of your body language. Crossed arms indicate a closed and defensive personality. Career experts advise that you keep your hands on the table in front of you.

- Make eye contact. Avoidance of eye contact can be interpreted as untrustworthiness.

- Stand and greet your interviewer with a firm handshake. A limp handshake or a bone crusher will be offensive to the interviewer.

- Nod occasionally while listening to indicate that you are attentive and alert.

- Think before answering and have a clear understanding of the question. If you don't understand a question, ask the interviewer for clarification.

- Keep your responses to two to three minutes. Stay on the point you were asked.

- Make sure you know what is on your resume.

- Wait for the interviewer to end the interview. Sometimes interviewees overlook this point and end the interview prematurely.

- End on an assumptive note, indicating that you feel you are a good fit for the position and how you can make a strong contribution to the organization.

- Inquire about the next step in the hiring process.

- Ask for a business card. This will provide you with the necessary contact information to send a thank-you note.

- Thank the interviewer even if he or she does not seem interested in you for the position. You are thanking the interviewer for his or her time.

After the Interview

Evaluate your interview performance. Interviewing is a skill that improves with practice. Learn from your mistakes and your strengths for the future.

Following each interview, it is important to send a thank-you note. This is considered protocol and a courtesy, and you are thanking the interviewers for their time, even if you do not receive a job offer. Whether you send a hard copy or e-mail is your personal preference. Of course, e-mail is faster, but a handwritten note is considered more personal. Make use of the thank-you note as a reminder to the interviewer of the valuable traits you bring to the job. Do not miss another opportunity to market yourself.

Sample Thank-You Note Following an Interview

510 Main Avenue
Arlington, VA 22222
June 15, 20XX

Ms. Jane Martin
Deputy Assistant Secretary for Management and Budget
200 Constitution Avenue N.W.
Washington, DC 20210

Dear Ms. Martin:

Thank you for your time in interviewing me for the position of Budget Analyst. As I mentioned during the interview, I am quite interested in the position, and I believe I have the right mix of skills and personality to perform its responsibilities successfully.

In my current position as a Budget Assistant at the Department of Homeland Security, I help in the preparation of regular and special budget reports; analyze monthly department budgeting; and provide advice and technical assistance with cost analysis, fiscal allocation, and budget preparation. In previous jobs, I have helped review operating budgets to analyze trends affecting budget needs, as well as examined budget estimates for completeness, accuracy, and conformance with procedures and regulations.

I am quite skilled at public speaking and have participated in Toastmasters International for a number of years. As a result, I have been called on to conduct briefings at all levels of management as well as train new staff to the office.

Again, thank you for considering me for the position. If I may provide any additional information, please feel free to contact me at (555) 555-1212 or at mjones@hmail.com.

Sincerely,

Matthew Jones

Matthew Jones

Types of Interview Questions

This section discusses types of interview questions in more detail and gives examples to help you prepare for interviews.

Behavioral and Competency Questions

The primary purpose of behavioral questions is to gather information from job candidates about their actual behavior during past experiences that demonstrate the competencies required for the job. The underlying premise of behavioral and competency questions is that the best predictor of future behavior on the job is past behavior under similar circumstances.

Question Example

Describe a situation in which you dealt with individuals who were difficult, hostile, or distressed. Who was involved? What specific actions did you take and what was the result?

Answer Example

As a claims representative for the Social Security Administration, I dealt with the aged, people with disabilities, and their caretakers.

Our payment system was electronic, and typically when changes were made, the person would receive an incorrect payment the following month. It often took two months for the system to update properly.

Oftentimes our clients could not comprehend the way SSA's electronic systems worked. When errors were made, clients sometimes came to the office overly irritated. They viewed SSA as purposely allowing the error to take place.

One of my responsibilities was to help clients calm down so they could understand the situation and help me to resolve it. My technique was simple, yet effective. When a person came into the office feeling distressed, I carefully listened to the problem without interrupting, unless I felt the person was further agitating himself or herself by talking about it too long. Tact and diplomacy were my mainstays in keeping the person from escalating his or her agitation. I had to intuitively know when the person had said enough to feel listened to and know when no positive purpose would be served by further discussing the situation. Most of the time clients calmed down on their own because they felt their concerns were being heard.

After listening carefully, my next step was to validate the person's feelings, not the situation. I said something like "Yes, Mr. Smith, I can understand how you might feel that way. However, I believe the problem might possibly be with the system. Would you be willing to review the situation with me so we can identify the problem and fix it?" Much of the time the problem was with the payment system.

On average one to two highly agitated clients came to the office each month. My approach worked about 99 percent of the time. Clients seemed relieved to learn that I was willing listen to them and then to work collaboratively to solve the problem. By validating the person's concerns, yet not allowing them to escalate, a client could learn to see me as an advocate. Clients were better served though my use of this approach.

I remember one time, however, where my approach only served to agitate the person even further. At that time, I knew I had done my best, and I asked my supervisor for help.

When my supervisor came, she used the same technique as I had, but for whatever reason, the client responded positively to her. After he became calm, the client was able to work with us to resolve his payment issue.

Sample Behavior-Based Interview Questions

- Describe a situation in which you were able to use persuasion to successfully convince someone to see things your way.

- Describe a time when you were faced with a stressful situation that demonstrated your coping skills.

- Give me a specific example of a time when you used good judgment and logic in solving a problem.

- Give me an example of a time when you set a goal and were able to meet or achieve it.

- Tell me about a time when you had to use your presentation skills to influence someone's opinion.

- Give me a specific example of a time when you had to conform to a policy with which you did not agree.

- Please discuss an important written document you were required to complete.

- Tell me about a time when you had to go above and beyond the call of duty to get a job done.

- Tell me about a time when you had too many things to do and you were required to prioritize your tasks.

- Give me an example of a time when you had to make a split-second decision.

- What is your typical way of dealing with conflict? Give me an example.

- Tell me about a time you were able to successfully deal with another person even when that individual may not have personally liked you (or vice versa).

- Tell me about a difficult decision you've made in the past year.

- Give me an example of a time when something you tried to accomplish failed.

- Give me an example of when you showed initiative and took the lead.

- Tell me about a recent situation in which you had to deal with a very upset customer or co-worker.

- Give me an example of a time when you motivated others.

- Tell me about a time when you delegated a project effectively.

- Give me an example of a time when you used your fact-finding skills to solve a problem.

- Tell me about a time when you missed an obvious solution to a problem.

- Describe a time when you anticipated potential problems and developed preventive measures.

- Tell me about a time when you were forced to make an unpopular decision.

- Please tell me about a time when you had to fire a friend.

- Describe a time when you set your sights too high (or too low).

Sample Competency-Based Interview Questions

- Attention to detail: Describe a project where your attention to detail kept the organization from making a big mistake.

- Communication: Describe an unpopular decision you had to make and how you handled implementing it.

- Conflict management: Describe a time where you found yourself working with someone who didn't like you. How did you handle it?

- Leadership: Describe a time when you exhibited participatory management.

- Planning, organizing, goal setting: Describe a time when you had to complete multiple tasks. What method did you use to manage your time?

- Presentation: Tell me about a time when you developed a lesson, training, or briefing and presented it to a group.

- Continuous learning: Tell me about a time when you recognized a problem as an opportunity.

- Customer service: Tell me about a recent situation in which you had to deal with a very upset customer or co-worker.

- Decisiveness: Tell me about a time when you had to stand up for an unpopular decision you made.

- Problem-solving: Describe a time when you analyzed data to determine multiple solutions to a problem. What steps did you take?

- Resource management: Describe a time when you capitalized on an employee's skill.

- Teamwork: Describe a time when you had to deal with a team member who was not pulling his or her weight.

Situational Questions

In contrast to behavioral questions, the questions in a situational interview are based on future-oriented behavior. These questions provide you with realistic job scenarios or dilemmas and ask how you would respond. The underlying premise is that a person's intentions are closely tied to his or her actual behavior.

Question Example

A very angry client walks up to your desk. She says she was told your office sent her an overdue check five days ago. She claims she has not received the check. She says she has bills to pay, and no one will help her. How would you handle this situation?

Answer Example

Having effectively dealt with this issue in the past, I would probably handle it similarly in the future. When I worked for the Social Security Administration as a claims representative, I sometimes had clients with payment issues.

I typically listened carefully without interrupting the client, but I did not allow the client to escalate the situation by going on and on about it. Tact and diplomacy were my mainstays in these situations. I had to intuitively know when the person had said enough to feel listened to and when he or she was further agitating themselves by continuing to discuss it.

After listening carefully, I would validate the person's feelings without validating the situation. I might say something like "Yes, Mrs. Smith, I can understand how you feel that way. However, I believe the problem might be with the system. Would you be willing to wait until I review the system to see if we can identify the problem and fix it?" Much of the time the problem would be with the payment system.

However, this person's situation is unique because she clearly is facing an emergency. In such instances, I was able to use SSA's tracking system to verify that the person had not cashed the check, to make sure the signature on the check was not hers, and to issue an emergency check. Additionally, I kept a desktop card index with information on local resources for emergencies such as this.

Sample Situational Interview Questions

- You have been assigned the team leader position for a high-profile special study team. The team will be working on this project for approximately four months. How would you go about organizing the team and selecting the team members?

- Your supervisor made a decision that you strongly disagree with. What approach would you use to discuss your position with your supervisor?

- You strongly believe in an idea you shared at a staff meeting. Your co-workers did not respond enthusiastically to it, and if you do nothing, your idea will in all likelihood be ignored. How will you go about making sure your idea will receive further consideration?

- Your supervisor is on vacation for a week. Before she left, she shared that she does not want to be contacted while she is away—under any circumstances. You were given a special assignment to complete during that time, which she asked you to have on her desk the day she returns. You hit a snag the second day your supervisor is gone. You cannot progress any further without receiving specific information that is known only to your supervisor. How would you handle this situation?

- Your work team has been assigned to implement the recommendations of a special study team. You understand
  some of the recommendations, but some are vague and
  open to interpretation. What process would you use to
  clarify the recommendations so they would be implemented properly?

Illegal Interview Questions and How to Handle Them

Sometimes illegal questions are asked out of ignorance on the
interviewer's part. Many illegal questions that are asked are
usually inadvertent, yet they can place you in an uncomfortable, delicate situation.

Title VII of the Civil Rights Act, the Age Discrimination in
Employment Act of 1967, and the Americans with Disabilities
Act regulate the questions employers can ask. Illegal or inap-
propriate interview questions ask about the following:

- Birthplace, ancestry, or national origin

- Race

- Physical disability, health, or medical history

- Marital status, children, or pregnancy

- Religion or religious days observed

- Gender

- Age

- Sexual preference

It's up to you on how to respond to such a question. Suggestions include

- Answer it. But be comfortable providing the information, because it may have repercussions in the future.

- Refuse to answer a question. Explain to the interviewer that the question appears to be illegal or is not relevant to the job. While you may risk losing out on the job, consider whether you want to work in an environment that seems to disregard civil rights.

- Do not answer the question directly, yet respond to its meaning. If you are asked, for example, "Do you have children?" you could say, "If you are wondering if I can travel, know that nothing will keep me from performing the job."

- Ignore the question and proceed to the next topic. If the question was an innocent lapse by the interviewer, he or she will be grateful that you handled it without risking the interview.

Source: www.gsworkplace.lbl.gov/DocumentArchive/ BrownBagLunches/IllegalorInappropriateInterviewQuestions. pdf

Using Informational Interviews to Your Advantage

An informational interview is an oft-underutilized tool that can help you make a decision about the applicability of a potential job to your career goals, as determined by your career exploration. Rather than rely solely on a job description, vacancy announcement, or rumor, in an informational interview you speak with someone who is performing work that is the same or similar to the job you want. In an informational interview, you learn about experiences of someone in the occupation, guided by questions that you create and ask.

Not to be confused with a selection interview, an informational interview is intended solely to obtain information. And, unlike a selection interview, it is virtually stress-free. There is no judging or rating involved. You are merely asking questions of someone who performs in a capacity that interests you. Prepare to spend 20–30 minutes interviewing the person you have selected as representative of your target job or organization. Beforehand, develop a list of questions with the intent to elicit information to help you make a decision.

Ideally, you will meet your contact face-to-face so you can see the work environment as well as establish an in-person connection. However, if a meeting is not possible, many job seekers have conducted their interviews by telephone and e-mail. As long as you have prepared questions that you are familiar with and comfortable asking, a phone or e-mail informational interview can benefit you. The important factor is gaining information.

Benefits of an Informational Interview

Some reasons to set up an informational interview include to

- Learn about an occupation you may be considering.
- Obtain pointers on how to prepare for a career.

- Find out about the culture of an organization you are thinking about pursuing.

- Focus on an occupational specialty.

- Develop confidence by getting feedback from a professional on your resume and qualifications.

- Get the inside scoop on the realities of a particular job or industry.

- Develop new networking contacts for future insight and guidance.

Finding People to Approach for an Informational Interview

You can find the right people to approach for informational interviews in a variety of ways:

- If you have a particular federal agency in mind, consider exploring its website. The organizational chart can provide you with the names and locations of individuals with the qualifications to provide the information you are seeking.

- Talk to people you know (that is, network) to find out who works in an industry or agency you wish to learn more about.

- If you are still in school or are a member of your school's alumni association, your career center may be able to provide names of graduates who work in the occupation you are interested in pursuing and who may be willing to grant informational interviews.

- Review professional association membership directories.

Requesting an Informational Interview

You can request an informational interview in several ways. Which method you choose may depend on your personality and comfort level.

- Telephone call. Requesting an informational interview via the telephone is somewhat akin to making a cold call, and it can be stressful. Be prepared, perhaps with a short script you have written and rehearsed, to quickly outline who you are and what you are requesting. Be clear that you are *not* looking for a job but seeking information.

- Personal introduction. If you found the name of the person you wish to interview through your network, perhaps you can ask your contact for a personal introduction. Conceivably your contact can call ahead on your behalf and let the potential interviewee know to expect your request for an interview.

- Letter or e-mail. This can be the best way to approach the person to both save time as well as give the person a chance to truly consider your request. If you received the person's name from a mutual acquaintance or your alma mater, be sure to mention that at the beginning of your note.

Sample Letter Requesting an Informational Interview

35 Tidewater Road
Clarksville, MD 21029
March 22, 20XX

Mr. Fred Martinez, Deputy Director
Office of Financial Management
DHHS/Office of the Assistant Secretary for Public Health
5600 Fishers Lane
Rockville, MD 20857

Dear Mr. Martinez:

I am currently working as a Budget Analyst and am considering a move to a federal agency doing the same kind of work. I have always had an interest in public health issues, and I would like to speak with you about how your work supports public health.

I graduated from the University of Montana, and I found your name on the list of alumni of note. The career center informed me that you have granted informational interviews in the past to individuals who seek career guidance.

Hopefully, you will be able to spend 20 minutes answering some questions I have about working in the public health system and the best way to pursue a federal career. I can send you my questions prior to our appointment if you would find that helpful. I will call you on Wednesday to set up an appointment.

Thank you very much for your time and for considering my request.

If I may provide any additional information, please feel free to contact me at (555) 555-1212 or at mhsmith@hmail.com.

Sincerely,

Mary Smith

Mary Smith

Making the Most of an Informational Interview

It is important that you know what you would like to learn before you set up an informational interview. People are busy, and you do not want to waste an individual's time by requesting and participating in this interview without being prepared. Following are suggested steps to maximize your time with the person who has agreed to meet with you.

- Research. Know something about the agency and industry you wish to explore. Your research doesn't need to be extensive, but it will show that you have taken the initiative to find information that you'd like your contact to elaborate on. In addition, developing questions is easier when you have a bit of information to jump-start the process.

- Develop questions. The most important aspect of preparing for the interview is to spend time developing questions based on your reasons for seeking information about the occupation, industry, or agency. The next section lists suggested questions to get you started. Of course, you will want to ask questions that pertain directly to your motivations and interests.

- Treat the informational interview like a job selection interview. Respect the contact's time, dress appropriately, and be professional. Follow the suggestions in "During the Interview" earlier in this chapter for additional guidance.

- Send a thank-you note following the interview.

- Keep the contact informed of your career progress. For example, if you apply to a management development program based on the suggestion of your contact, let him or her know.

In an informational interview, you are the interviewer. Therefore, you will take the lead and monitor the time. If you requested 20 minutes for the interview, make sure you do not exceed that time unless your contact indicates that additional time is acceptable. It is advisable to ask for the names of other people to get in touch with for other informational interviews. Be sure to ask your contact if you can use his or her name when setting up other interviews.

Sample Questions for Informational Interviews

Here are some sample questions for informational interviews:

- What is it about this job that you like most?
- What is it about this job that you like least?
- What types of training would you recommend that someone with my background take to prepare for the type of work you do?
- What is the advancement potential in this career?
- What types of tasks do you perform on a regular basis?
- Are you given authority to make decisions in your job?
- I like to work independently, with minimal supervision. Is that realistic in this job?
- How did you learn about this career?
- Does your manager allow for professional development?

- Would you choose this occupation/job/organization if you were just starting your career?

- Do you have a flexible schedule? Do you work weekend and evening hours?

- Is telecommuting an option in your job or with this organization?

- What is the impact of your work on the mission of the organization?

Taking the Next Steps After Informational Interviews

When you have completed the informational interview, you should spend some time processing the information you have received as part of your career exploration. Organize your thoughts, ideas, and impressions of what you heard and perhaps develop additional questions for other interviews. Experts suggest that you conduct several informational interviews to confirm information as well as to obtain a variety of perspectives and ideas.

Closing Points

This book has paved the way for you to create and maintain a clear vision of your federal career. You have identified and distinguished yourself, and you are now prepared to pursue the work that you were meant to do as a federal public servant.

Congratulations!

SKILLS ASSESSMENT

I n chapter 3, you are asked to consider your special skills. The following competency assessment will reveal your top skills.

Competency Assessment

Adapted with permission from pages 55–58 of *Your Career Planner*, 10th Edition, by Borchard et al. Copyright © 2008 by Kendall Hunt Publishing Co.

To be completed after finishing this assessment.

List your top three competencies. If you want to develop any new competencies, list them under desired rating:

My **Assessment** Rating   My **Desired** Rating

1. _____   _____

2. _____   _____

3. _____   _____

ASSESSMENT DIRECTIONS

According to the **Rating Key** below, assess your current level of competency in the following skills and abilities:

Rating Key

0 = Can**not** use this skill/ability at all

1 = Can **minimally** use this skill/ability

2 = Can **moderately** use this skill/ability

3 = Can **considerably** use this skill/ability

4 = Can **extensively** use this skill/ability

Add the number of checks you made (separately) in each column, multiply by the number at the top of the column, and place those totals in the subtotal row. Then add the subtotal amounts and list the total below the table.

Interpersonal/People	0	1	2	3	4
Listening skillfully/understanding meaning					
Developing rapport					
Counseling/helping/guiding/mentoring					
Drawing people out/interviewing					
Instructing/training/educating					
Social grace/putting others at ease					
Group facilitating					
Communicating tactfully					
Being of service/responding					
Providing information/advising					
Cooperating with others					
Showing warmth and concern					
Being supportive or cooperative					
Healing/nursing/nurturing/curing					
SUBTOTAL					

Interpersonal/People TOTAL: _____

Analytical/Researching	0	1	2	3	4
Analyzing/diagnosing					
Researching/investigating					
Interpreting data					
Classifying/organizing/systematizing					
Evaluating/assessing					
Scientific/technical writing					
Logical decision making and problem solving					

(continued)

Rating Key:

0 = **Cannot** use this skill/ability at all. 1 = Can **minimally** use this skill/ability. 2 = Can **moderately** use this skill/ability. 3 = Can **considerably** use this skill/ability. 4 = Can **extensively** use this skill/ability.

(continued)

Analytical/Researching	0	1	2	3	4
Financial analysis					
Mathematical/numerical reasoning					
Using facts/evaluating					
Separating important from unimportant facts					
Prioritizing facts, figures, or information					
Scientific curiosity					
Using logic or rational reasoning					
SUBTOTAL					

Analytical/Researching TOTAL: _____

Detail/Data	0	1	2	3	4
Working with data					
Proofreading/editing					
Inspecting/examining/inventorying					
Word processing/typing					
Following directions/procedures accurately					
Being careful/exacting					
Quickly/correctly solving basic math					
Scheduling/organizing events or activities					
Accounting/keeping track of data					
Categorizing/sorting					
Remembering numbers or specific facts					
Attending to details					
Filing/classifying/recording/retrieving					
Completing assignments on time					
SUBTOTAL					

Detail/Data TOTAL: _____

Rating Key:
0 = Can**not** use this skill/ability at all. 1 = Can **minimally** use this skill/ability. 2 = Can **moderately** use this skill/ability. 3 = Can **considerably** use this skill/ability. 4 = Can **extensively** use this skill/ability.

Innovative/Original	0	1	2	3	4
Using your imagination to create					
Graphic designing					
Using intuition					
Designing programs, events, activities					
Creating ideas					
Acting/performing					
Creative writing/self-expression					
Brainstorming possibilities					
Artistic sense/aesthetics					
Drawing/artistic designing					
Creative movement/dancing					
Synthesizing ideas/facts in new ways					
Being innovative					
Composing music, songs, lyrics					
SUBTOTAL					

Innovative/Original TOTAL: _____

Manual/Technical	0	1	2	3	4
Assembling/installing					
Constructing/building					
Fixing/repairing					
Manual dexterity					
Working with animals					
Using hand tools					
Operating machinery/equipment					
Driving vehicles—trucks, tractors, forklifts, buses					
Moving materials by hand					

(continued)

Rating Key:

0 = Can**not** use this skill/ability at all. 1 = Can **minimally** use this skill/ability. 2 = Can **moderately** use this skill/ability. 3 = Can **considerably** use this skill/ability. 4 = Can **extensively** use this skill/ability.

(continued)

Manual/Technical	0	1	2	3	4
Horticulture skills—working with plants					
Landscaping and grounds keeping					
Physical stamina					
Outdoor labor					
Mechanical reasoning					
SUBTOTAL					

Manual/Technical TOTAL: _____

Managing/Influencing	0	1	2	3	4
Administering a program or resources					
Directing/supervising others					
Making decisions quickly					
Negotiating/contracting with others					
Persuading/influencing/selling					
Overseeing programs/projects/activities					
Planning/goal setting					
Undertaking entrepreneurial activities					
Organizing/managing an activity, task, or project					
Convincing others through force of personality					
Taking risks					
Completing deals or transactions					
Coordinating people and activities					
Exercising group leadership					
SUBTOTAL					

Managing/Influencing TOTAL: _____

Rating Key:

0 = Can**not** use this skill/ability at all. 1 = Can **minimally** use this skill/ability. 2 = Can **moderately** use this skill/ability. 3 = Can **considerably** use this skill/ability. 4 = Can **extensively** use this skill/ability.

Return to the beginning of this appendix and list your three highest rated competency areas. Now take a second look and decide whether you would like to develop any other competencies. List them under your desired rating in order of preference.

O*NET JOB SUMMARY REPORT

As explained in chapter 5, O*NET OnLine at www.onetonline.org provides summary reports for occupations. Here is an example of the report for budget analysts. You can use a summary report when researching a job to help determine if it is right for you.

Summary Report for Budget Analysts

Examine budget estimates for completeness, accuracy, and conformance with procedures and regulations. Analyze budgeting and accounting reports for the purpose of maintaining expenditure controls.

Sample of reported job titles: Budget Analyst, Budget Officer, Budget and Policy Analyst, Chief Financial Officer (CFO), Cost Accountant, Staff Analyst, Accounting Supervisor, Budget Coordinator

Tasks

Direct the preparation of regular and special budget reports.

Analyze monthly department budgeting and accounting reports to maintain expenditure controls.

Provide advice and technical assistance with cost analysis, fiscal allocation, and budget preparation.

Examine budget estimates for completeness, accuracy, and conformance with procedures and regulations.

Summarize budgets and submit recommendations for the approval or disapproval of funds requests.

Review operating budgets to analyze trends affecting budget needs.

Consult with managers to ensure that budget adjustments are made in accordance with program changes.

Compile and analyze accounting records and other data to determine the financial resources required to implement a program.

Perform cost-benefit analyses to compare operating programs, review financial requests, or explore alternative financing methods.

Tools & Technology

Tools used in this occupation: Desktop computers, laser printers, notebook computers, personal computers

Technology used in this occupation:

Accounting software — Deltek Costpoint; Hyperion Enterprise

Database user interface and query software — Microsoft Access; online analytical processing OLAP software; relational database software; structured query language SQL

Enterprise resource planning ERP software — Lilly Software Associates VISUAL Enterprise; Microsoft Dynamics GP; NetSuite NetERP; Sage Active Planner

Financial analysis software — Budget monitoring systems; Microsoft FRx; Oracle Corporate Performance Management CPM software; Satori Group proCube software

Presentation software — Microsoft PowerPoint; SAP Crystal Xcelsius

Time accounting software — Payroll software; time and attendance software; Valiant Vantage

Knowledge

Economics and Accounting — Knowledge of economic and accounting principles and practices, the financial markets, banking, and the analysis and reporting of financial data.

English Language — Knowledge of the structure and content of the English language, including the meaning and spelling of words, rules of composition, and grammar.

Mathematics — Knowledge of arithmetic, algebra, geometry, calculus, statistics, and their applications.

Administration and Management — Knowledge of business and management principles involved in strategic planning, resource allocation, human resources modeling, leadership technique, production methods, and coordination of people and resources.

Computers and Electronics — Knowledge of circuit boards, processors, chips, electronic equipment, and computer hardware and software, including applications and programming.

Clerical — Knowledge of administrative and clerical procedures and systems, such as word processing, managing files and records, stenography and transcription, designing forms, and other office procedures and terminology.

Law and Government — Knowledge of laws, legal codes, court procedures, precedents, government regulations, executive orders, agency rules, and the democratic political process.

Personnel and Human Resources — Knowledge of principles and procedures for personnel recruitment, selection, training, compensation and benefits, labor relations and negotiation, and personnel information systems.

Skills

Active Listening — Giving full attention to what other people are saying, taking time to understand the points being made, asking questions as appropriate, and not interrupting at inappropriate times.

Reading Comprehension — Understanding written sentences and paragraphs in work-related documents.

Critical Thinking — Using logic and reasoning to identify the strengths and weaknesses of alternative solutions, conclusions, or approaches to problems.

Judgment and Decision Making — Considering the relative costs and benefits of potential actions to choose the most appropriate one.

Complex Problem Solving — Identifying complex problems and reviewing related information to develop and evaluate options and implement solutions.

Mathematics — Using mathematics to solve problems.

Writing — Communicating effectively in writing as appropriate for the needs of the audience.

Active Learning — Understanding the implications of new information for both current and future problem-solving and decision-making.

Abilities

Mathematical Reasoning — The ability to choose the right mathematical methods or formulas to solve a problem.

Number Facility — The ability to add, subtract, multiply, or divide quickly and correctly.

Written Comprehension — The ability to read and understand information and ideas presented in writing.

Oral Comprehension—The ability to listen to and understand information and ideas presented through spoken words and sentences.

Oral Expression—The ability to communicate information and ideas in speaking so others will understand.

Problem Sensitivity—The ability to tell when something is wrong or is likely to go wrong. It does not involve solving the problem, only recognizing there is a problem.

Deductive Reasoning—The ability to apply general rules to specific problems to produce answers that make sense.

Written Expression—The ability to communicate information and ideas in writing so others will understand.

Inductive Reasoning—The ability to combine pieces of information to form general rules or conclusions (includes finding a relationship among seemingly unrelated events).

Work Activities

Getting Information—Observing, receiving, and otherwise obtaining information from all relevant sources.

Interacting with Computers—Using computers and computer systems (including hardware and software) to program, write software, set up functions, enter data, or process information.

Analyzing Data or Information—Identifying the underlying principles, reasons, or facts of information by breaking down information or data into separate parts.

Processing Information—Compiling, coding, categorizing, calculating, tabulating, auditing, or verifying information or data.

Communicating with Supervisors, Peers, or Subordinates—Providing information to supervisors, co-workers, and subordinates by telephone, in written form, by e-mail, or in person.

Organizing, Planning, and Prioritizing Work—Developing specific goals and plans to prioritize, organize, and accomplish your work.

Making Decisions and Solving Problems—Analyzing information and evaluating results to choose the best solution and solve problems.

Establishing and Maintaining Interpersonal Relationships—Developing constructive and cooperative working relationships with others, and maintaining them over time.

Interpreting the Meaning of Information for Others—Translating or explaining what information means and how it can be used.

Job Zone

Job Zone Four: Considerable Preparation Needed

Education. Most of these occupations require a four-year bachelor's degree, but some do not.

Related Experience. A considerable amount of work-related skill, knowledge, or experience is needed for these occupations. For example, an accountant must complete four years of college and work for several years in accounting to be considered qualified.

Job Training. Employees in these occupations usually need several years of work-related experience, on-the-job training, and/or vocational training.

Job Zone Examples. Many of these occupations involve coordinating, supervising, managing, or training others. Examples include accountants, sales managers, database administrators, teachers, chemists, environmental engineers, criminal investigators, and special agents.

Education

Percentage of Respondents	Education Level Required
65	Bachelor's degree
15	Master's degree
8	High school diploma or equivalent

Interests

Interest code: CEI

Conventional—Conventional occupations frequently involve following set procedures and routines. These occupations can include working with data and details more than with ideas. Usually there is a clear line of authority to follow.

Enterprising—Enterprising occupations frequently involve starting up and carrying out projects. These occupations can involve leading people and making many decisions. Sometimes they require risk taking and often deal with business.

Investigative—Investigative occupations frequently involve working with ideas, and require an extensive amount of thinking. These occupations can involve searching for facts and figuring out problems mentally.

Work Styles

Attention to Detail — Job requires being careful about detail and thorough in completing work tasks.

Integrity — Job requires being honest and ethical.

Analytical Thinking — Job requires analyzing information and using logic to address work-related issues and problems.

Dependability — Job requires being reliable, responsible, and dependable, and fulfilling obligations.

Cooperation — Job requires being pleasant with others on the job and displaying a good-natured, cooperative attitude.

Initiative — Job requires a willingness to take on responsibilities and challenges.

Independence — Job requires developing one's own ways of doing things, guiding oneself with little or no supervision, and depending on oneself to get things done.

Stress Tolerance — Job requires accepting criticism and dealing calmly and effectively with high-stress situations.

Work Values

Working Conditions — Occupations that satisfy this work value offer job security and good working conditions. Corresponding needs are Activity, Compensation, Independence, Security, Variety, and Working Conditions.

Support — Occupations that satisfy this work value offer supportive management that stands behind employees. Corresponding needs are Company Policies, Supervision: Human Relations, and Supervision: Technical.

Independence — Occupations that satisfy this work value allow employees to work on their own and make decisions. Corresponding needs are Creativity, Responsibility, and Autonomy.

Related Occupations

11-3011.00 Administrative Services Managers

13-1023.00 Purchasing Agents, Except Wholesale, Retail, and Farm Products

13-1051.00 Cost Estimators

13-1111.00 Management Analysts

13-2011.01 Accountants

13-2011.02 Auditors

15-2011.00 Actuaries

15-2031.00 Operations Research Analysts

19-3011.00 Economists

Wages & Employment Trends
National

Median wages (2009)	$32.05 hourly, $66,660 annual
Employment (2008)	67,000 employees
Projected growth (2008–2018)	Faster than average (14% to 19%)
Projected job openings (2008–2018)	22,300
Top industries (2008)	Government, Educational Services

SAMPLE VACANCY ANNOUNCEMENT

Job Title: MANAGEMENT ANALYST

Department: Department of Housing and Urban Development

Agency: Federal Housing Commissioner, Assistant Secretary for Housing

Job Announcement Number: HII-DE-495123-2YW

SALARY RANGE: $89,033.00–$115,742.00/year

OPEN PERIOD: Wednesday, January 12, 20XX, to Thursday, January 27, 20XX

SERIES & GRADE: GS-0343-13

POSITION INFORMATION: Full-time career/career conditional

PROMOTION POTENTIAL: 14

DUTY LOCATIONS: 1 vacancy—Washington, DC, metro area

WHO MAY BE CONSIDERED: United States citizens

JOB SUMMARY: Our mission focuses on expanding home ownership, increasing access to affordable housing, strengthening communities through economic development, fighting housing discrimination, and tackling homelessness issues.

Join the Department of Housing and Urban Development (HUD) team if you are looking for a challenging career opportunity and want to be an impact player helping individuals achieve the American dream! HUD is an integral partner in revitalizing and improving communities across America.

Office address: HQ HUD, 451 Seventh Street S.W., Washington, DC. To learn more about HUD's mission and programs, go to www.hud.gov.

Federal status candidates may apply for this position under announcement #F11-MP-494975-2YWz. Candidates who want to apply under a special non-competitive hiring authority, such as Schedule A, must apply under the federal status announcement.

KEY REQUIREMENTS:

- You must be a U.S. citizen to apply for this position.
- This announcement may be used to fill more than one vacancy.
- A background investigation is required for all federal employees.
- Must meet specialized experience requirements (see Qualifications).

MAJOR DUTIES: This position is located in the Office of Single Family Housing. The incumbent reports directly to the Associate Deputy Assistant Secretary for Single Family Housing and assists with administrative, procurement, and management information activities relating to headquarters and field operations. The incumbent works directly with and receives assignments from the Senior Management Analyst and other designated staff persons who have pivotal roles in Single Family's procurement processes and activities. Incumbent uses automated systems to collect, report, and interpret procurement management information and is responsible for developing spreadsheets, charts, and reports as needed by Single Family management and submissions to the Department.

QUALIFICATIONS AND EVALUATIONS

QUALIFICATIONS REQUIRED:

GS-13: You qualify at the GS-13 grade level if you possess one year of specialized experience equivalent to the GS-12 grade level in the federal government. Specialized experience includes experience such as performing duties related to the analysis and evaluations of management operations for an organization; using analytical methods for studies and projects related to management improvement, productivity improvement, management controls coordination, or long-range planning; participating in development of operating manuals and directives covering administrative functions of an organization.

EDUCATIONAL SUBSTITUTION: There is no educational substitution at this grade level.

Completion of the occupational/assessment questionnaire is required. It measures your ability to demonstrate the following knowledge, skills, and abilities. Provide specific examples of your qualifications and significant accomplishments in your resume.

Skill in the use of Microsoft software packages and data management systems to develop spreadsheets, manipulate data, prepare reports and presentations within the procurement related process

Ability to analyze issues/problems and recommend solutions

Skill in written communications

Skill in verbal communications

HOW YOU WILL BE EVALUATED: Once the application process is complete, a review of your application will be made to ensure you meet the job requirements. To determine if you are qualified for this job, a review of your resume and supporting documentation will be made and compared against your responses to the occupational questionnaire. The numeric rating you receive is based on your responses to the questionnaire and any supporting narrative. The score is a measure of the degree to which your background matches the knowledge, skills, and abilities required of this position that are listed below. If, after reviewing your resume and/or supporting documentation, a determination is made that you have inflated your qualifications and/or experience, your score can and will be adjusted to more accurately reflect your abilities. Please follow all instructions carefully. Errors or omissions may affect your rating.

CATEGORY RATING procedures will be used to rank qualified candidates. Candidates will be ranked into three categories: Best, Better, and Good. You will be assigned the appropriate quality level based on your responses in the occupational questionnaire.

Best category: Highly proficient in all the knowledge, skills, and abilities of the job as demonstrated by occupational questionnaire and resume; candidates can perform effectively in the position almost immediately or with a minimum of training/orientation.

Better category: Highly proficient in some, but not all, of the knowledge, skills, and abilities of the job as demonstrated by occupational questionnaire and resume; candidates will be able to perform effectively in the position with training/orientation.

Good category: An overall basic level of knowledge, skills, and abilities of the job as demonstrated by occupational questionnaire and resume; candidates may need extensive training/orientation to perform successfully in the job.

Application of Veterans' Preference: Category rating and selection procedures place those with veterans' preference above non-veterans within each category. Veterans who meet the eligibility and qualification requirements, and who have a compensable service-connected disability of at least 10 percent, are listed in the highest quality category (Best Qualified).

BENEFITS AND OTHER INFO

BENEFITS: HUD offers a generous compensation package that may include such benefits as the following: competitive salaries; health, dental, vision, and life insurance plans; paid leave and holidays; telecommuting or other flexible work schedules; transit subsidies; Student Loan Repayment Program; retirement investment options (401[k]-type plan); Flexible Spending Accounts; long-term-care insurance; and child-care subsidies.

OTHER INFORMATION:

This position is **Exempt** from the Fair Labor Standards Act, as amended.

This position is **NOT** in the bargaining unit.

Payment of relocation expenses is **NOT** authorized.

A Confidential Financial Disclosure Report (SF-450) will be required for certain positions. You may be asked to complete the necessary Financial Disclosure Report to meet that requirement.

Travel requirements: Occasional.

HUD is a smoke-free environment.

A background security investigation is required for all federal employees. Appointment will be subject to the applicant's successful completion of the security investigation and favorable adjudication. Failure to meet these requirements will be grounds for termination. If you are considered for selection, you will be required to complete the Declaration of Federal Employment to determine your suitability for federal employment and to authorize a background investigation.

Candidate selected may be required to serve a one-year probationary period.

If position has been identified as a Testing-Designated position under HUD's Drug-free Workplace Plan, any individual tentatively selected that does not currently occupy a Testing-Designated position will be required to submit to urinalysis to screen for illegal drug use prior to appointment.

If you are a displaced federal employee, you may be entitled to receive special priority selection under the Interagency Career Transition Assistance Program (ICTAP) or the Agency Career Transition Assistance Program (CTAP). To receive this priority consideration you MUST submit a copy of the appropriate documentation such as a RIF separation notice, Standard Form 50, Notification of Personnel Action, stating that you were separated by RIF, or a letter from OPM or your agency documenting your priority consideration status with your application package. You must be applying for a position at or below the grade level of the position from which you have been separated, and the position must not have greater promotion potential than the position from which you were separated. You must be applying for a position in the same local commuting area from which separated. You must provide all required information specified in the vacancy announcement, e.g. narrative statements, appraisals, etc. Failure to comply with ALL of the instructions in the vacancy announcement will result in non-consideration for the vacancy. Additionally, you must be determined to be Well-Qualified for the position. Well-Qualified means an eligible employee who meets all eligibility and qualification requirements (including any selective placement factors) and obtains at least 80 points out of 100 quality ranking factor points that can be awarded during the ranking process.

HUD employees are prohibited from owning Fannie Mae and Freddie Mac securities and from owning or acquiring property subsidized by Section 8 tenancies. HUD employees are also prohibited from the active participation in a business dealing with or related to real estate. This includes the sale and management of real estate. These interests are prohibited under the HUD Supplemental Standards of Conduct regulation at 5 CFR 7501. Certain HUD employees are required to file a financial disclosure report.

Due to our security procedures, our office will not accept any applications submitted via email or standard mail.

Selective Service: If you are a male applicant born after December 31, 1959, you must certify that you have registered with the Selective Service System or are exempt from having to do so under the Selective Service Law.

Veterans' Preference: If you are entitled to veterans' preference, you should indicate the type of veterans' preference you are claiming on your resume. Your veterans' preference entitlement will be verified by the employing agency.

- For 5-point veterans' preference, please provide your DD-214 (Certificate of Release or Discharge from Active Duty), official statement of service from your command if you are currently on active duty, or other official documentation (e.g., copy of military orders, campaign documents, or expeditionary award citation, etc.) that proves your military service was performed under honorable conditions.

- For 10-point veterans' preference, please submit a Standard Form (SF) 15, Application for 10-Point Veteran Preference, and the required documentation.

HOW TO APPLY: To apply for this position, you must provide a complete application package that includes your resume, complete occupational/ assessment questionnaire, and additional required documents (see Required Documents section below). The complete application package must be submitted by 11:59 PM (EST) on Saturday, July 02, 20XX.

TO BEGIN THE PROCESS, click the Apply Online button to create an account or log in to your existing USAJOBS account. Follow the prompts to complete the occupational/assessment questionnaire. Please ensure you click the Submit My Answers button at the end of the process.

Note: To check the status of your application or return to a previous or incomplete application, log in to your USAJOBS account, select Application Status, and click on the more information link under the application status for this position.

To fax supporting documents you are unable to upload, complete the cover page at http://staffing.opm.gov/pdf/usascover.pdf using the following Vacancy ID: 495123. Fax your documents to 1-478-757-3144.

If you cannot apply online

1. Click the link to view and print the occupational/assessment questionnaire,

2. Print the 1203FX form to provide your response to the occupational questionnaire, and

3. Fax the completed 1203FX form along with any supporting documents to 1-478-757-3144. Your 1203FX will serve as a cover page for your fax transmission.

REQUIRED DOCUMENTS: Resume or application; response to the occupation/assessment questionnaire; Veterans' Preference documentation (DD-214 or equivalent, SF-15, and VA Letter, as appropriate). PLEASE SUBMIT ONLY the requested/required documents. Failure to provide required documents will be disqualifying under the competitive process. PLEASE DO NOT MAIL your application package.

WHAT TO EXPECT NEXT: After the announcement has closed, we will conduct an evaluation of your eligibility and qualifications and determine your ranking. The most highly qualified candidates will be referred to the hiring manager for further consideration and possible interview.

ASSESSMENT QUESTIONS: Management Analyst. Vacancy ID: 495123 Announcement Number: H11-DE-495123-2YW USAJOBS Control Number: 2305864

Occupational/Assessment Questions:

1. Instructions: Select the one statement below that best describes your specialized experience to meet the basic requirements for this position at the GS-13 grade level.

A. I have one full year of specialized experience equivalent in difficulty and complexity to the work performed at the GS-12 level (the next lower grade in the federal service), which has equipped me with the particular knowledge, skills, and abilities to successfully perform the duties of the position. My experience includes analytical and evaluative methods for making recommendations for resolution of administrative management issues and improvement of overall program and operational effectiveness, statistical survey and analysis work, and administering an organizational segment and its work programs.

B. I do not have experience as a Management Analyst as listed above.

In the next section, you are asked to provide your level of proficiency on the knowledge, skills, and abilities for this position. When making your ratings, please do not overstate or understate your level of experience and capability. You should be aware that your ratings are subject to further evaluation and verification. Deliberate attempts to falsify information will be grounds for not selecting you or for dismissing you from employment with the organization. For each factor, select the ONE response that most accurately describes your current level of experience and capability. Please ensure that your resume can support your selection.

A. I have no experience in performing this work behavior.

B. I have limited experience in performing this work behavior. I have had exposure to this work behavior but would require additional guidance, instruction, or experience to perform it at a proficient level.

C. I have experience performing this work behavior across routine or predictable situations with minimal supervision or guidance.

D. I have performed this work behavior independently across a wide range of situations. I have assisted others in carrying out this work behavior. I seek guidance in carrying out this work behavior only in unusually complex situations.

E. I am considered an expert in carrying out this task. I advise and instruct others in carrying out this work behavior on a regular basis. I am consulted by my colleagues and/or superiors to carry out this work behavior in unusually complex situations.

2. Uses Microsoft software packages and data management systems in order to develop spreadsheets, manipulate data, and prepare reports and presentations.

3. Develops procedures and systems for establishing, operating, and assessing the effectiveness of administrative control systems.

4. Prepares graphs and charts that present clear, concise, and effective analytical results of evaluations and studies performed.

5. Conducts complex and special studies for efficiency and productivity.

6. Recommends changes or improvements in work methods and procedures.

7. Researches new or improved business and management practices for application to programs and operations.

8. Prepares written communication such as technical reports and evaluations.

9. Develops procedures, guides, or handbooks.

10. Composes correspondence for high-level officials.

11. Represents management in meetings, workshops, and conferences.

12. Conducts formal presentations.

13. Explains technical or complex information to managers and customers.

FEDERAL JOB SEARCH INFORMATION FOR SPECIAL POPULATIONS

T his appendix offers federal jobs information for people with disabilities, veterans, ex-offenders, and students.

People with Disabilities

Of 2 million-plus federal employees, more than 209,284 have documented disabilities. That is approximately 7 percent of the federal civilian workforce, a rate which has remained relatively constant since 1980. All federal agencies are required by law to develop outreach efforts to identify qualified candidates that will help the agency to meet its workforce diversity goals, and individuals with disabilities are included in that population.

Agencies, to the extent permitted by law, are directed to increase use of the federal government's excepted service hiring authority for persons with disabilities and increase participation of individuals with disabilities in internships, fellowships, and training and mentoring programs.

Individuals interested in special appointments with the federal government must be proactive and begin networking with local agencies, contacting listed resources, and aggressively seeking all federal employment opportunities. Find a list of agency Selective Placement Program Coordinators to contact at http://apps.opm.gov/sppc_directory/. Additionally, OPM provides federal application information for people with disabilities at http://golearn.gov/HiringReform/

applicant/hpd.htm. More information about the application process for people with disabilities appears at www.opm.gov/disability/.

Agency personnel offices work with State Vocational Rehabilitation Agencies, the Department of Veterans Affairs, colleges and universities, and other organizations to identify qualified people with disabilities. Hiring may be accomplished through the competitive hiring process or, if the qualifications are met, through the use of excepted service appointment regulations. All federal agencies are able to use excepted service hiring regulations for the disabled, which is the path many people with disabilities take to get hired by the federal government.

A good number of people with disabilities start their federal career in the excepted service, yet most federal jobs are in the competitive service. In the competitive service, individuals compete for positions using their federal resumes and application essays. The result is that individuals are placed on a certificate of eligibles in rank order of their rating. Hiring managers can select from the top three candidates on the list. A competitive service job ensures federal career status. Unfortunately, many special appointments through excepted service are temporary. In addition, people under excepted service appointments do not acquire federal career status. However, these folks sometimes get converted to career status after two years of satisfactory performance.

Individuals with mental retardation or severe physical or psychiatric disabilities can receive an appointment through an excepted service program; learn more at www.opm.gov/disability/hrpro.asp. Because appointments of people with severe physical disabilities are excepted service appointments, agencies may accept resumes without posting job notices. Applicants should indicate "5 CFR 213.3102(u)" on their resumes.

Certification

An individual who has a physical disability is considered to have met OPM qualification standards for either a temporary competitive service appointment or an excepted service appointment when an appropriate certification is received from a State Vocational Rehabilitation Agency or the Department of Veterans Affairs. The certification is prepared by a counselor on the basis of job-site inspection, analysis of job tasks, and evaluation of the proposed appointee's abilities and disabilities.

The certification required for an excepted service Schedule A appointment of an individual who is mentally retarded need only state that the individual has the ability to perform the duties of the position, is physically able to do the job safely, and can maintain himself or herself in the work environment.

The certification required for appointment of individuals with psychiatric disabilities under an excepted appointment must include documentation of a history of mental illness that includes hospitalization or outpatient treatment within the previous two years, a statement by a psychologist or psychiatrist on the individual's capability to function in the work setting, and a statement indicating that the individual is unemployed or has had a significant period of substantially disrupted employment within the previous two years.

30 Percent or More Disabled Veterans

Federal employers may give a noncompetitive temporary appointment of more than 60 days or a term appointment to a veteran retired from active military service with a disability rating of 30 percent or more or rated by the VA within the preceding year as having a compensable service-connected disability of 30 percent or more. The appointee must meet all qualification requirements. The agency may convert the employee to a career or career-conditional appointment at any time during the employee's temporary or term appointment.

Disabled veterans who are eligible for training under the VA vocational rehabilitation program may enroll for training or work experience at an agency under the terms of an agreement between the agency and VA. If the training is intended to prepare the individual for eventual appointment in the agency rather than just work experience, the agency must insure that the training will enable the veteran to meet qualification requirements for the position. A certificate of training on successful completion allows any agency to appoint the veteran noncompetitively that may be converted to career or career-conditional at any time.

The Department of Homeland Security Wounded Warrior Program recruits and hires severely wounded veterans. Learn more at www.dhs.gov/xabout/careers/gc_1257434968190.shtm.

Special Accommodations

OPM uses special examination (testing) procedures for applicants who are physically handicapped to assure that their abilities are properly and fairly assessed. When federal agencies hire a person with disabilities, efforts are made to remove or modify barriers to his or her ability to effectively perform the essential duties of the position.

Sample Cover Letter for Disabled Excepted Service Applicant

Date

Applicant Contact Information
Name
Address, City, State, Zip
Phone/email address

Agency Information
Name
Contact's Title
Street Address,
City, State, Zip

Dear Mr./Ms. (person's last name only):

First paragraph: I am an individual with a disability according to 5 CFR 213.3102 (u). I am eligible to apply for federal employment under the Schedule A hiring authority, Appointment for Persons with Disabilities. I am forwarding my application to be considered for _____ (position title, grade, vacancy number).

Second paragraph: Explain the skills and experiences you have that will make you successful in the position. Talk about classes you have taken and volunteer experiences that are related to the position. Do not repeat your resume; highlight related accomplishments. The goal is to show the employer that you have confidence in your ability to succeed in the position.

Third paragraph: Demonstrate that you have done some research about this agency. This research does not have to be extensive, but it shows that you have taken some time to think about this position and put some effort into this letter. This makes a very good impression on employers.

Fourth paragraph: State that you would welcome an interview to discuss this opportunity. You might mention that if you do not hear anything from the potential employer in two to three weeks, you will call to see where they are in the process. Finish by thanking the person for his or her attention and express a desire to meet the person in the near future.

Sincerely,
Sign name
Typed name

Note: The number of paragraphs is optional.

Veterans

Each federal agency lists Veteran Employment Program Offices responsible for promoting veterans' recruitment, employment, training and development, and retention. Veterans are encouraged to contact individuals on the list for employment opportunities. Find the list at www.fedshirevets.gov/AgencyDirectory/index.aspx.

Special Hiring Authorities for Veterans will enhance your job search. OPM encourages job-seeking veterans to ask for consideration under as many hiring authorities as they are eligible for, in addition to claiming their veterans' preference under the competitive examining process (if applicable). To provide acceptable documentation of your preference or appointment eligibility, the member 4 copy of your DD214, "Certificate of Release or Discharge from Active Duty," is preferable. If you are claiming 10-point preference as a disabled veteran, you need to submit an "Application for 10-point Veterans' Preference." Learn more about Special Hiring Authorities for Veterans at www.fedshirevets.gov/job/shav/index.aspx.

Ex-Offenders

According to the U.S. Bureau of Justice Statistics, each year more than 650,000 men and women are released from federal and state prisons. Unfortunately for these ex-offenders, no special programs bring them into the federal workforce. According to the Bureau of Prisons's Employment Information Handbook, www.bop.gov/inmate_programs/emp_info_handbk.pdf, ex-offenders should use USAJOBS for their federal job search and apply using the competitive process shared in this book. Some non-federal resources for ex-offenders include the Fortune Society (http://fortunesociety.org/), *Best Resumes and Letters for Ex-Offenders* by Wendy Enelow, and *The Ex-Offender's Job Hunting Guide* by Ron Krannich.

Students and Recent Graduates

President Obama issued Executive Order (EO) 13562 to enhance the recruiting and hiring of students and recent graduates. The EO addresses problems recent graduates have had in trying to secure a job with the federal government.

According to EO 13562, "The existing competitive hiring process for the federal civil service...is structured in a manner that, even at the entry level, favors job applicants who have significant previous work experience. This structure, along with the complexity of the rules governing admission to the career civil service, creates a barrier to recruiting and hiring students and recent graduates."

The EO consolidates student and recent graduate programs into the Pathways Programs framework with three clear program paths tailored to recruit, train, and retain well-qualified candidates. The Internship Program, Recent Graduates Program, and Presidential Management Fellows Program will be collectively known as the Pathways Programs. The Pathways Programs will provide noncompetitive conversion eligibility to federal employment status and will be used to develop talent for civil service careers. EO 13562 also eliminates the Federal Career Intern Program. OPM says it will provide assistance for agencies in adopting the reforms by 2012. Learn more at the following websites:

www.whitehouse.gov/the-press-office/2010/12/27/executive-order-recruiting-and-hiring-students-and-recent-graduates

www.chcoc.gov/transmittals/
TransmittalDetails.aspx?TransmittalID=3418

Sampling of Federal Jobs by College Major

To help you choose the right field, USAJOBS provides a table that groups federal jobs often filled by college graduates with appropriate academic majors. The jobs listed under each major are examples and not an all-inclusive list. Note that many jobs do not require a degree; job-related experience is just as good. You can qualify for a large number of administrative jobs with a degree in any academic major. To illustrate this point, the list leads off with some popular jobs for which any major is qualifying. For a longer list, see www. usajobs.gov/EI/jobsbycollegemajor.asp#icc.

ANY MAJOR
Administrative Officers
Civil Rights Analysts
Contract Representatives
Environmental Protection
Logistics Management
Management Analysts
Personnel Occupations
Public Affairs
Supply Management
Writers and Editors

ACCOUNTING
Accountants
Auditors
Financial Institution Examiners
Internal Revenue Agents

AGRICULTURE
Agricultural Commodity Graders
Agricultural Engineers
Soil Scientists

AGRONOMY
Agronomists
Soil Conservationists
Soil Scientists

ANTHROPOLOGY
Anthropologists
Museum Curators

ARCHEOLOGY
Archaeologists
Museum Curators

ARCHITECTURE
Architects
Construction Analysts
Landscape Architects
Naval Architects

ARTS, FINE AND APPLIED
Exhibits Specialists
Illustrators
Photographers

ASTRONOMY
Astronomers and Space Scientists
Geodesists

AVIATION
Air Navigators
Air Traffic Controllers
Aviation Safety Inspectors

BIOLOGY
Entomologists
Fishery Biologists
Zoologists

BOTANY
Agronomists
Botanists
Forestry Technicians
Horticulturists

BUSINESS
Budget Analysts
Import Specialists
Internal Revenue Officers

CARTOGRAPHY
Cartographers
Geodetic Technicians

CHEMISTRY
Chemists
Consumer Safety Officers
Toxicologists

COMMUNICATIONS
Communications Specialists
Public Affairs Specialists
Technical Writers and Editors

CORRECTIONS
Correctional Institution Administrators
Correctional Officers

COUNSELING
Educational Services Specialists
Personnel Specialists
Psychologists

CRIMINAL JUSTICE/LAW ENFORCEMENT
Border Patrol Agents
Criminal Investigators
Internal Revenue Officers

DIETETICS AND NUTRITION
Dietitians
Food Technologists
Nutritionists

ECONOMICS
Actuaries
Budget Analysts
Financial Analysts

EDUCATION
Educational Program Specialists
Public Health Educators
Training Instructors

ELECTRONICS TECHNOLOGY
Communications Specialists
Electronics Technicians
Patent Examiners

EMPLOYEE/LABOR RELATIONS
Employee Relations Specialists
Labor Relations Specialists
Workers Compensation Claims
  Examiners

ENGINEERING (ANY SPECIALTY)
Civil Engineers
Electrical Engineers
Industrial Engineers
Nuclear Engineers

ENGLISH AND LITERATURE
Public Affairs Specialists
Technical Writers and Editors
Writers and Editors

ENVIRONMENTAL STUDIES
Ecologists
Environmental Health Technicians
Fish and Wildlife Refuge Management

EPIDEMIOLOGY
Environmental Health Technicians
Microbiologists

FINANCE
Appraisers and Assessors
Budget Analysts
Financial Analysts
Tax Examiners

FISH, GAME, AND WILDLIFE MANAGEMENT
Fish and Wildlife Refuge Management
Game Law Enforcement Agents
Wildlife Biologists

FOOD TECHNOLOGY AND SAFETY
Consumer Safety Inspectors
Dietitians and Nutritionists
Food Technologists
Toxicologists

FOREIGN LANGUAGE
Border Patrol Agents
Equal Employment Opportunity
  Specialists
Foreign Affairs Specialists

FORESTRY
Fish and Wildlife Refuge Management
Foresters
Soil Conservationists

GEOGRAPHY
Cartographers
Geographers

GEOLOGY
Geodesists
Hydrologists
Oceanographers

GEOPHYSICS
Geophysicists

HEALTH
Environmental Health Technicians
Health Physicists

HISTORY
Archivists
Intelligence Specialists
Museum Curators

HOME ECONOMICS
Consumer Safety Officers
Food Technologists

HORTICULTURE
Horticulturists

HOSPITAL ADMINISTRATION
Health System Administrators
Public Health Programs Specialists

HUMAN RESOURCE
MANAGEMENT
Equal Employment Opportunity
  Specialists
Human Resource Specialist

HYDROLOGY
Environmental Engineers
Hydrologists

INDUSTRIAL MANAGEMENT
Industrial Property Managers
Production Controllers
Quality Assurance Specialists

INFORMATION TECHNOLOGY
Computer Programmers
Computer Specialists

INSURANCE
Crop Insurance Administrators
Social Insurance Claims Examiners

INTERNATIONAL RELATIONS
Foreign Affairs Specialists
Intelligence Specialists
Public Affairs Specialists
Trade Specialists

JOURNALISM
Printing Specialists
Public Affairs Specialists
Technical Writers and Editors
Writers and Editors

LAW
Administrative Law Judges
Attorneys
Legal Instruments Examiners
Patent Attorneys

LAW ENFORCEMENT
Alcohol, Tobacco, and Firearms
  Inspectors
Border Patrol Agents
Criminal Investigators
Police Officers

LIBERAL ARTS/HUMANITIES
Contact Representatives
Customs Inspectors
Management Analysts
Program Analysts

LIBRARY SCIENCE
Librarians
Library Technicians
Medical Record Librarians

MANAGEMENT
Administrative Officers
Management Analysts
Program Analysts

MANAGEMENT, FACILITIES
Correctional Institution Administrators
Facility Managers
Industrial Property Managers

MANAGEMENT INFORMATION
SYSTEMS
Computer Science Specialists
Computer Specialists
Management Analysts
Operations Research Analysts

MARKETING
Contract Specialists
Packaging Specialists
Trade Specialists

MATHEMATICS
Actuaries
Cartographers
Computer Science Mathematical
  Statisticians
Statisticians

MEDICAL SUPPORT
Diagnostic Radiological Technicians
Medical Technicians
Nuclear Medicine Technicians
Therapeutic Radiological Technicians

METEOROLOGY
Meteorologists

NATURAL RESOURCE
MANAGEMENT
Wildlife Biologists
Wildlife Refuge Management

NURSING
Nurses
Physician's Assistants

PARK AND RECREATION MANAGEMENT
Foresters
Outdoor Recreation Planners
Park Rangers

PHARMACY
Consumer Safety Inspectors
Pharmacists
Pharmacologists

PHYSICAL EDUCATION
Corrective Therapists
Outdoor Recreation Planners
Recreation Specialists

PHYSICAL SCIENCE
Metallurgists
Physicists

PHYSICS
Astronomers and Space Scientists
Health Physicists
Physicists

POLITICAL SCIENCE/ GOVERNMENT
Foreign Affairs Specialists
Public Affairs Specialists
Social Scientists

PSYCHOLOGY
Employee Development Specialists
Psychologists

PUBLIC ADMINISTRATION
Budget Analysts
Employee Relations Specialists
Management Analysts

PUBLIC HEALTH
Environmental Health Technicians
Food Inspectors
Public Health Educators

PUBLIC RELATIONS
Foreign Affairs Specialists
Public Affairs Specialists

PURCHASING
Contract Specialists
Purchasing Specialists

REAL ESTATE
Building Managers
Realtors

REHABILITATION THERAPY
Corrective Therapists
Manual Arts Therapists
Physical Therapists

SOCIAL WORK
Recreation Specialists
Social Scientists
Social Workers

SOCIOLOGY
Social Scientists
Sociologists

STATISTICS
Actuaries
Statisticians
Transportation Industry Analysts

SURVEYING
Geodesists
Land Surveyors

SYSTEMS ANALYSIS
Computer Science Specialists
Management Analysts

THEOLOGY
Chaplains
Social Workers

TRANSPORTATION
Highway Safety Specialists
Transportation Industry Analysts
Transportation Operators

ZOOLOGY
Animal Scientists
Zoologists

FOR ADDITIONAL INFORMATION

Chapter 2: The Federal Government as an Employer

Federal Employment Information Fact Sheets: Benefits of Working for the Federal Government at www.usajobs.gov/ei/benefits.asp

Chapter 3: Knowing Yourself

Keirsey assessment on temperament: www.keirsey.com

SCANS skills information: www.soicc.state.nc.us/soicc/planning/skillsjob.htm. SCANS is an acronym for the Secretary's Commission on Achieving Necessary Skills, which was created by the Department of Labor to study the skills needed in the American workplace.

50 Best Jobs for Your Personality by Laurence Shatkin

What's Your Type of Career?: Unlock the Secrets of Your Personality to Find Your Perfect Career Path by Donna Dunning

Do What You Are: Discover the Perfect Career for You Through the Secrets of Personality Type by Paul D. Tieger and Barbara Barron

Chapter 4: Developing Your Career Identity

Personal branding: www.williamarruda.com

Meaningful work: www.utne.com/Spirituality and www.ericmaisel.com

Personal mission statement: www.quintcareers.com/creating_personal_mission_statements.html and http://literacy.kent.edu/Oasis/Leadership/mission.htm

Find your calling: www.fastcompany.com/magazine/13/hbrplus.html, www.changingcourse.com, and www.encore.org

What Color Is Your Parachute? by Richard Nelson Bolles

The Motivation to Work by Frederick Herzberg, Bernard Mausner, and Barbara Bloch Snyderman

First Things First by Steven Covey

Chapter 5: Introducing Federal Departments and Agencies and Federal Jobs

Mission-critical jobs listed by the Partnership for Public Service: http://data.wherethejobsare.org/wtja/home

OPM Standing Registers Agency Guidance: www.chcoc.gov/Transmittals/Attachments/trans2916.pdf

Guide to America's Federal Jobs by Karol Taylor and Janet M. Ruck

Chapter 6: Skills the Federal Government Is Seeking

Office of Personnel Management Talent Management System: www.opm.gov/hcaaf_resource_center/6-1.asp

Chapter 7: Finding Your Fit in the Federal Government

Partnership for Public Service resource for federal careers by field of interest: www.makingthedifference.org/federalcareers/careersbyinterest.shtml

Chapter 8: Closing Your Skills Gap

Department of Education on Finding Schools that Match Interests and Goals: www2.ed.gov/students/prep/college/consumerinfo/finding.html

Chapter 9: Creating Your Career Plan

Goal setting: www.goal-setting-for-success.com

Motivation: www.1000ventures.com/business_guide/crosscuttings/motivating_yourself.html and www.selfgrowth.com/motivation.html

The Psychology of Winning by Denis Waitley

What They Don't Teach You at Harvard Business School by Mark McCormack

Taming Your Gremlin by Rick Carson

Chapter 10: The Federal Job Application Process

Virginia Tech Career Services resource about federal government employment at www.career.vt.edu/FederalGovernmentEmployment/FederalEmploymentIndex.html#major

Chapter 11: Interviewing for a Federal Job

Informational interviews: www.bls.gov/opub/ooq/2002/summer/art03.pdf

Structured interviews: http://apps.opm.gov/ADT/ContentFiles/SIGuide09.08.08.pdf

INDEX

FDIC (Federal Deposit Insurance Corporation), 71
federal agencies, 69–75
  Congressional Budget Office, 69–70
  Corporation for National and Community Service, 70
  Defense Applicant Assistance Office, 70
  Environmental Protection Agency, 70
  Equal Employment Opportunity Commission, 70
  Export-Import Bank of the United States, 71
  Federal Communications Commission, 71
  Federal Deposit Insurance Corporation, 71
  Federal Emergency Management Agency, 71
  Federal Energy Regulatory Commission, 71–72
  Federal Reserve System, 72
  General Services Administration, 72
  Government Accountability Office, 72
  Library of Congress, 72–73
  mission statement, reviewing, 95–96
  National Aeronautics and Space Administration, 73
  Nuclear Regulatory Commission, 73
  Office of Management and Budget, 74
  Office of Personnel Management, 74
  Office of the Director of National Intelligence, 73–74
  Securities and Exchange Commission, 74
  The Smithsonian Institution, 75
  Social Security Administration, 75
  strategic plans, reviewing, 97–98
  United States Agency for International Development, 75
  website for information, 95
Federal Communications Commission, 71
federal departments, 63–69
  Agriculture, 64
  Commerce, 64
  Defense, 64–65
  Education, 65
  Energy, 65
  Health and Human Services, 65–66
  Homeland Security, 66
  Housing and Urban Development, 66
  Interior, 66–67
  Justice, 67
  Labor, 67
  State, 67–68
  Transportation, 68
  Treasury, 68
  Veterans Affairs, 69
Federal Deposit Insurance Corporation, 71
Federal Emergency Management Agency, 71

federal employees, benefits for, 11–14
Federal Employees Retirement System (FERS), 13
Federal Energy Regulatory Commission, 71–72
federal government, branches of, 9
federal job seekers, common mistakes of, 2–7
federal jobs
  application process
    cover letter, writing, 149–151
    for ex-offenders, 226–227
    hiring reform, 145–146
    for people with disabilities, 222–226
    personal essay, writing, 157–162
    resume, writing, 152–156
    for students and recent graduates, 227
    vacancy announcements, 146–148
    for veterans, 226
  availability of, 8
  categories of, 9–10
  interviews
    common interview questions, 187–194
    illegal interview questions, 194–195
    importance of, 170–171
    informational interviews, 195–202
    preparation for, 177–183
    types of, 171–176
  listed by college major, 227–231
  location of, 15
  networking strategies, 162–167
    creative networking, 164–165
    online support groups, 166–167
    social networking, 166–167
  occupational series, 11
  sample vacancy announcement, 215–221
  skills needed for
    ECQs (Executive Core Qualifications), 84–90
    fundamental competencies, 83–84, 89–90
  summary report for budget analysts, 208–214
  top 10 federal occupations, 100–123
    Administration and Program Staff, 106–108
    Business and Industry Specialist, 116–119
    Contract Specialist, 114–116
    Engineer, General, 119–121
    Human Resources Specialist, 122–123
    Information Technology Management Specialist, 101–104
    Management and Program Analyst, 104–106
    Medical Officer, 109–110
    Nurse, 110–111
    Office Clerk/Assistant, 111–113
  top fields for, 78–81

Praise for *Find Your Federal Job Fit*

"Ruck and Taylor have said what the American workforce needs to hear: The conventional wisdom about 'getting into the government and then transferring to something you like' doesn't work. This little book shows you how to analyze your skills, experience, and values. It introduces you to the mission and values of key federal departments and agencies. And it tells you how to create a match between you and a target job destination. When you have worked your way through this book, you'll never again think of federal employment as that giant place where you get in and then worry about the fit later. You can get it right from the beginning."

—Anne S. Headley, MA, NCC, NCCC, career counselor
in private practice, University Park, MD

"Teaches how to find a suitable federal job and successfully fill out the necessary application forms. But the book offers much more. Readers who complete its carefully crafted exercises, based on sound career development theory, will learn about self, clarify values, and accent skills....Good for everyone who wants to be guided toward meaningful work."

—Lee J. Richmond, Ph.D., Professor of Education, Loyola
University Maryland; licensed psychologist; and career consultant

"An extremely valuable resource for anyone contemplating a career with the federal government. A careful reading of the book and doing the useful activities equips job seekers with an understanding of where within this huge bureaucracy to find a fit for their unique strengths, how to credibly prepare and present themselves, and how to avoid the mistakes that could undermine their candidacy. I plan to recommend this invaluable resource to my clients looking to pursue a career in the federal government."

—David C. Borchard, Ed.D., author of *Joy of Retirement:
Finding Happiness, Freedom, and the Life You've Always Wanted*

"Take the mystery out of your federal job search! Taylor and Ruck guide you through the unique aspects of the federal hiring process. In chapter 5, their description of federal departments and what each one does gives you an invaluable overview of possibilities. Their tips on the federal job application process are the best ones around. And do check out their excellent advice on networking in the federal arena."

—Lynne Waymon, CEO of Contacts Count, LLC, and co-author of *Make Your Contacts Count,* Second Edition

"Finally a single publication focused to truly assist individuals who wish to secure a position with the federal government.... The exercises assist in identifying what strengths, interests, and abilities bring them comfort, satisfaction, and a sense of accomplishment. These activities are critical to real success for long-term career efforts and pride in their roles....The authors tested their approaches repeatedly before and during the writing of this book....As a former federal employee who has worked with six major federal agencies and all 10 independent agencies, this is the first book I feel comfortable recommending without qualification."

—James P. Dittbrenner, author of *Career Fairs and Open Houses—Mid-Atlantic Newsletter*

"Combines solid career development tools with federal government information...truly helps you to target your best matches and achieve your objective of having a federal career, not just a job."

—Annabelle Reitman, Ed.D., career management strategist and author

"Thorough and comprehensive...immediately applicable to exponentially enhancing one's federal job search efforts."

—Natalie Kauffman, career consultant, KauffmanNcareers, LLC

"Absolutely superb in clarifying what you want and how to get there in the federal job maze....For anyone who is overwhelmed by the federal application process, this is the book that changes the paradigm."

—Marvin Adams, certified career coach